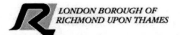

THE
WILD THINGS
GUIDE TO

THE CHANGING PLANT LIFE OF THE BRITISH ISLES

THE
WILD THINGS
GUIDE TO

THE CHANGING PLANT LIFE OF THE BRITISH ISLES

DR TREVOR DINES

WITH SALLY EATON AND CHRIS MYERS

4
Books

To Nev – thanks for keeping it all together.
Diolch.

FRONTISPIECE A windswept Scots pine (Pinus sylvestris)
stands proud above a sea of heather (Calluna vulgaris)
in the New Forest National Park, Hampshire, southern
England. In our wildlife-rich landscape every plant,
great or small, has a story to tell (see pp.140, 143, 219).

BELOW AND OPPOSITE A haze of yellow buttercups
(Ranunculus acris) and various grasses abound in a
meadow in Essex, southeast England. Fifty years ago,
such wildflower meadows were common across our
countryside.

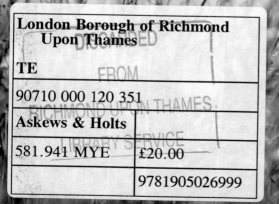

CONTENTS

FOREWORD

BELOW Although nettles can sting, they're not all bad, as their leaves sustain the caterpillars of many butterflies. Nettles are also good indicators of nutrient-rich soil, high in phosphate and nitrogen.

BOTTOM Chris Myers has roamed the green hills of his home turf on the Yorkshire Dales, northern England, all his life. Designated a National Park in 1954, the Dales provide a haven for plants and all forms of wildlife.

It's not every day that you're asked to describe the redeeming qualities of a nettle but that day came for me and, happily enough, I do think that nettles are great and didn't mind the bother of doing so. So there I was, on my home turf in the Yorkshire Dales and up to my armpits in nettles *(Urtica dioica)*; only I had a television camera for company – and quite a big one at that. I later learned that this was what television people call a screen test, so I had one without really realizing it and I suspect that the nettles were probably the stars of the show. But those lovely stinging clumps of green started something – my test with the nettles led to a part in the *Wild Things* series that's been a year-long, cross-country trail of discovery, all about finding, foraging, rooting and rummaging.

I'm a garden designer by trade and I've always been fascinated by the world outside and what's growing in it. I'm one of those outdoor sorts who needs a 'fresh-air fix' every day and I'd usually much rather be out walking the lanes, striding the hills or mucking about on my in-laws' farm than being cooped up indoors. Cities have their limits for me and I can only stay in them for just so long before I'm dying to be home again, where I can soak up my surroundings. I'm lucky to live somewhere that I love and to have grown up seeing the seasons turn, and experiencing that very subtle beat of nature's changing calendar. At home I fish, I roam, I wander and I never stop looking. All that ferreting about outdoors somehow seems to have left its mark on me and fuelled my curiosity about the natural world.

Mother nature is a marvellous thing – she's cheeky and changeable, sometimes shy, sometimes subtle. Poking around in hedgerows at the side of paths or in old stone walls allows me to discover just what she's getting up to next. I've done it since I was a kid and I do much the same today. It's like going on nature's own treasure hunt, when I get to discover what's living in every tiny crevice and corner. When I don't know what I've found, I go home, look it up and learn something new. Every day is part of an unfolding story that just never ends. The time spent in that great big wild backyard is what inspires my designs and ideas for the show gardens that I enter into competitions (see pp.190–1). So, being asked to join a television series to go and hunt down what's creeping, crawling and climbing through our countryside seemed

like that day among the nettles – my idea of all right; and it turned out that the television series wasn't just about the glamorous, fluffy stuff, but about getting stuck into plenty of foliage too.

During a remarkable twelve-month quest tracking down our photosynthesizing friends and all the other weird and wonderful wildlife that they harbour, I've come to appreciate that the wild things really are all around us, whether they're tiddlers, such as Danish scurvygrass (*Cochlearia danica*), or massive, spreading thugs, such as rhododendron (*Rhododendron x superponticum*). Along the way, I discovered many surprising things, such as the fact that there are miniature waterbears (tardigrades) living in Birmingham and that plants can travel at high speed (see pp. 102–3, 114–15). I now realize that mother nature's booty might well be staring us right in the face; sometimes we just need to look a little more closely to see it.

Working on the *Wild Things* series alongside top botanist Dr Trevor Dines and lichenologist Sally Eaton, I've picked up a trick or two from my clever new friends and have really started to read the landscape in a whole new way.

That great big wild garden out there is changing every day. There's never been a better time to go out there and get to know it.

CHRIS MYERS

The Wild Things *team, Chris Myers (left), Dr Trevor Dines (middle), Sally Eaton (right) and Lottie the Labrador, set off on a voyage around the British Isles to find out exactly why our landscape and plant life have changed so dramatically over the past fifty years.*

OPPOSITE Bright pink thrift (Armeria maritima) clothes a clifftop on the eastern coast of Scotland, providing a sheltered spot for a herring gull nest.

BELOW Introduced from India in 1839, Himalayan balsam (Impatiens glandulifera) is a newcomer that's having a big impact today (see pp.180–2).

BOTTOM A large skipper butterfly searches for nectar in the flowers of viper's-bugloss (Echium vulgare) on Salisbury Plain in Wiltshire, southern England.

INTRODUCTION

Something remarkable is happening across the landscape of the British Isles today. If you think that the countryside and the world around you is not quite the same as it used to be, you'd be right. Nature is on the move – our wild things are wandering, changing home, coming and going across the landscape. Newcomers, such as Spanish bluebell (*Hyacinthoides hispanica*), are appearing in unexpected places, while old timers, such as corn buttercup (*Ranunculus arvensis*), are disappearing from view (see pp.34–5, 58–71).

The wild and the wonderful

Wherever you live – in city apartments or country cottages – and however unlikely it might seem that wild things flourish beside you, it's certain that, at this very moment, something large or small is creeping, crawling and making its way somewhere, not necessarily toward you but certainly toward ideal conditions in which to settle down and thrive. From the obvious to the microscopic, from giant oaks to miniature mosses, vibrant, living things are shuffling and shifting all around us. We just might not always realize quite how many or how varied they are, how they got where they are today, or what exactly they're doing here. Now, though, we're starting to want to know more about the wild things that live alongside us.

Originally, in our early past, we had a much closer relationship with the natural world. For centuries, we lived off the land, explored and roamed through it, but somehow along the way we lost track of its natural rhythms and beat, its order and integration. Today, many of us would like to recover something of that lost connection with the land and discover what natural marvels lie just around the corner, over our own garden wall.

In other ways, too, our fascination with the wild and the wonderful, the free and the simple is clearly growing. Increasingly today, we're stepping back outside into the 'great outdoors' to explore what's lain beneath our feet all along – we're camping, glamping, foraging and slowly rediscovering the good life outdoors.

THE *WILD THINGS* TEAM

Chris Myers

**GARDEN DESIGNER • GOLD MEDAL WINNER •
NETTLE-LOVER**

For Chris, it all started with an old bath full
of swimming bugs, an allotment and a Polish
granddad who could pickle, preserve and grow
almost anything. Mother nature was like an
extra member of the Myers family – there
were annual bilberry-picking forages, sibling
rivalries played out on the strawberry patch,
a family garden ripped up for planting veggies
and masses of time spent roaming, rambling
and poking around outdoors. Maybe it was a
foregone conclusion that at some point Chris
would have to get digging too.

The outdoor bug started with the weekly
adventure of going to his granddad's allotment.
It was a bit of a trek to get there but another,
wilder world lay in store. Hours would pass by
in which a grubby-kneed Chris would discover
a world of dirt, soil and stuff that grew. Slowly
but surely he learned a trick or two from his
grandfather who had come to the British Isles
after being injured in World War II (1939–45).
His granddad's example of growing his own
veggies rubbed off on young Chris – it wasn't
long before he had his own plot and was trying
to outsmart his sister with a bumper crop.

Growing up in rural Sutton in Craven, North
Yorkshire, northern England, Chris was able to
mooch about the countryside to his heart's
content. Poking his nose into the countryside
on his doorstep set him up with a lifelong
interest in discovering what was going on out
there in the wild. He became immersed in the
growing season and learnt what was coming
into flower and what was on its way out; he sat
by riverbanks and canals fishing; he explored
hedgerows and wandered off across the moors.
When he returned home with a ripe swag
of juicy bilberries after the summer forage, a

*Chris has always been passionate about nature and
life outdoors (top). Channel 4's* Wild Things *series
gave him the chance to inspect wild plants across the
country, including cornfield poppies (*Papaver rhoeas)
at Ranscombe Farm in Kent, southeast England (above).

marathon jam-making session would follow.
These early lessons in self-sufficiency gave Chris
a taste for life among the wild things, which in
turn shaped what he chose to do with his life.

Strangely, though, what came next was a brief
spell in turf management. It was prompted by
several family holidays spent abroad with an aunt
and uncle who managed swish golf courses. After
a stint helping out on the turf, Chris thought that
he might have discovered his niche, as well as a
way to earn a living outdoors – as a greenkeeper.

Back at home, he soon embarked on a three-year amenity horticulture course at Askham Bryan College in North Yorkshire. After college, though, he lasted only four months in his first job as a greenkeeper – sitting on a lawnmower and going round in circles just wasn't for Chris.

When a job as assistant head gardener on the Duke of Devonshire's Bolton Abbey Estate in the Yorkshire Dales followed, Chris was out of the world of grass and into a rich landscape of plants and other wild things. There was no looking back and, four years later, he moved on to become head gardener on a private 16-hectare estate.

It was at this point that Chris got involved in the world of show gardens and won his first Royal Horticultural Society (RHS) gold medal and Best in Show award at BBC Gardeners' World Live 2004 for his Waterscape garden, in which he had even built a life-sized canal as part of his showpiece (see p.190). Since then, Chris has gone on to win further acclaim and prizes. His Garden

of Natural Goodness at BBC Gardeners' World Live 2009 earned him another gold medal as did his Bodgery Garden in 2011, while At a Dale's Pace, which was inspired by his own home patch, won him a silver gilt medal at the RHS Tatton Show in 2005 (see pp.190–1).

All those years spent rummaging around outdoors discovering nature's wild treasures still play a key part in shaping the kind of gardens that Chris likes to design, which he now does full-time for a string of private clients.

Nature still never fails to amaze Chris, so taking 'just a bit of the wild' into the formal settings of competitions, such as Tatton Show, remains an ongoing mission, while trying to showcase nature's wild side in his designs continues to be his daily challenge. After all, this is a man who loves nettles and he's not afraid to grow them in his gardens.

Lottie, Chris's black Labrador, accompanies him to work and on his daily trips around the countryside.

TOP *A wood mouse feasts on hoarded berries and nuts in readiness for its winter hibernation.*

ABOVE *Sevenspot ladybirds chase large green nettle aphids on the underside of a nettle leaf. Despite their short legs, these ladybirds are good runners and voracious hunters.*

Our own wild backyard

The current move to look more closely at the extraordinary variety of wild things that live all around us, at the landscapes that stretch out in front of us and at the country through which we travel every day reflects a deeper desire to reconnect with mother nature at grassroots level in that vast wild garden out there – our own natural backyard.

Meeting today's growing interest in the natural world, both the television series *Wild Things* and this beautifully illustrated book, which accompanies it, open a window on to our green and pleasant land, revealing the wide diversity of wild things flourishing in the British Isles.

To investigate our countryside in greater depth, *The Wild Things Guide to the Changing Plant Life in the British Isles* begins from the ground up – quite literally, in fact – from where wild plants start growing at our feet. Just imagine for a moment a world without all the fluffy and cuddly things, without everything that waddles, tweets and hoots, and you'd still be left with an amazingly rich variety of life that continues creeping, climbing and growing, an arena of activity and industry – the world of plants. In many ways plants are the building blocks of nature, as a moment's reflection will quickly reveal, since it's easy to see that specific plants, such as grasses or trees, shape and colour almost every habitat, ranging from grasslands to woodlands, from moorlands to farmlands.

But plants are not just building blocks: they also provide essential shelter and vital food and oxygen for the wild things that they harbour (see p.43). In so many intriguing and unexpected ways, plants are the unspoken heroes of our countryside. They act as the resilient guardians of a multitude of wild things, and as the keepers of secret kingdoms, glimpsed only under the microscope. Vibrant, verdant and often brightly coloured, plants also add rich variety and contrast to the landscape. Without the plants, a whole swathe of colour would simply disappear.

Evidence from the cutting-edge

To discover exactly what's going on in the countryside today, *The Wild Things Guide* examines the most recent, ground-breaking scientific research that's been revealing the extent and scale of change in the natural world over the last half century. This new evidence stems from a unique natural history project, launched in 1950 by the Botanical Society of the British Isles (BSBI), in which thousands of botanists and volunteers have been gathering millions of records of plant life from all over the country. One of the largest natural history projects ever attempted, it's generated an illuminating series of maps that illustrate the exact distribution patterns of individual plants (see chapter 1).

First collected together in 1962 in the innovative *Atlas of the British and Irish Flora*, each plant map charts the spread – and sometimes the decline – of an individual wild plant in the British Isles. As the maps in the original *Atlas*, combined with its sequel of 2002, clearly illustrate which species are moving in or out of a particular area, they can provide a fresh perspective on the wider natural world. By comparing the distribution maps for plants and other wild things and by analysing the changes that have taken place since the start of the project, it's possible to piece together the stories of individual plants, which can in turn reveal the larger underlying patterns of movement across the natural world. To understand exactly how these revealing maps are produced and what clues they hold, turn to chapter 1.

Chalk downlands, such as Beacon Hill in Hampshire, southern England, are some of the best places to search for rare wild plants. With up to forty different species per 1sqm, including orchids (Orchidaceae), wild mignonette (Reseda lutea) and horseshoe vetch (Hippocrepis comosa), Beacon Hill is a magnet for nature lovers.

THE *WILD THINGS* TEAM

Dr Trevor Dines

PLANT EXPERT • MAP MAN • ORCHID-MAD

Finding a wild orchid at the tender age of twelve is one of the things that set this plant man on his path. It was an early purple orchid (*Orchis mascula*) and it was tucked away in a wood on the farm where he grew up in Hampshire, southern England. After making this first great find, Trevor cashed in his pocket money for a field guide to identify the plant properly and he's been ticking things off in his guidebook ever since.

Growing up amidst 607 hectares of farmland, with its meadows, trees and abundant hedgerows, provided the perfect wild back garden for someone with an eye for what was moving and growing. Trevor's outdoor obsessions ranged from collecting rocks, trying to catch bullhead fish by hand and spending hours watching rainbow trout patrol their patches. Much to his mother's exasperation, he even emptied his clothes drawer and turned it into a specimen cabinet showcasing all his latest finds. By the time he was thirteen years old, Trevor had used his now well-thumbed field

Trevor's fascination with wild plants started at an early age (above) as his twin and elder brother joined him on hunts for toadstools on the family farm. Today, Trevor's passion continues in his work to protect declining native species (below), such as juniper (Juniperus communis).

guide to tick off all the plants on the farm. He also had a thriving vegetable patch, was a dab hand with cacti and succulents and was the youngest member of the Wessex Orchid Society. Trevor now suspects that the raffles at their weekly meetings were probably fixed, as he always came home with a new orchid.

Given all this early rummaging and a natural green finger, it was no surprise that Trevor continued to be interested in the wonders of wildlife and the world beyond the garden wall, and went on to study plant life in more depth after school. It was, in fact, the pull of the plants that brought Trevor north to Snowdonia in Wales, where he read botany at Bangor University, later adding a PhD in plant architecture to his ever-expanding plant knowledge. The diverse landscape of Snowdonia, with its rolling mountains, isolated beaches and mass of wonderfully varied plants, fuelled and continues to inspire many of his wild plant hunts and investigations. Trevor came to Wales and he's never left.

It was on his home patch on a beach on the island of Anglesey, off the northwest coast of

Wales, that Trevor achieved a lifetime's ambition when he discovered and recorded an entirely new plant to science – the Anglesey horsetail. He named it *Equisetum x robertsii* after a local school teacher, Dick Roberts, an inspirational amateur botanist..

Travelling further afield, Trevor next collaborated on the Botanical Society of the British Isles' remarkable record of plant distribution, one of the biggest natural history projects of its kind (see pp.24–7). As co-author, Trevor scoured vast areas of the British Isles, recording plants as well as co-ordinating the collation of 9 million different records from volunteers all over the country, which culminated in the *New Atlas of the British and Irish Flora* (2002).

Trevor has also managed to find time to hot-air balloon over the rainforests of Cameroon, western Africa, to study tropical trees; and to go plant-hunting in Tibet and southeast Asia. His stomping ground, though, remains Wales where he currently works

As both a farmer's son and a botanist, Trevor well understands the need to find a balance between productive farming and a landscape rich in wildlife.

for Plantlife, the wild plant conservation charity. Here he has implemented the Back from the Brink Species Recovery Programme; developed a network of volunteer Flora Guardians who monitor plants on a regular basis; and published the first ever stock-take of all native plants in Wales, *A Vascular Plant Red Data List for Wales* (2008). Trevor also co-authored *The Ghost Orchid Declaration* (2010) and *Forestry Recommissioned: Revitalising the Woodlands of Wales* (2012).

Outside work, Trevor maintains a 1-hectare garden and is a founder and past chairman of the Friends of Treborth Botanic Garden in Bangor. He's also an avid road cyclist, swimmer, runner and hill walker in order to counter the effects of an unhealthy relationship with cakes. He considers his obsession with orchids entirely healthy.

ABOVE AND BELOW *The decline of many cornfield flowers (above), such as corn marigold (Chrysanthemum segetum), is a sign that the health of our countryside is changing. To find out why, the* Wild Things *team set out to explore the landscape (below).*

Deciphering the clues

As plants are the building blocks of most habitats, what happens to them may well hold the key to the health of our countryside. If plants are either increasing or decreasing, or moving in or out of an area, the multitude of other wild things that they support will be shifting with them. Being able to decipher the changing patterns of plant distributions can offer invaluable insights into events in the wider natural world. Spotting change at the outset, such as the decline of a cornfield flower, can alert us to the potential knock-on effects elsewhere in the natural world, such as a corresponding decrease in certain bees (see pp.42, 212–14). Tracking down the roots of change, whether triggered by natural or man-made causes, can help highlight essential facts about the wild things.

Our wild team

To help spot the clues in the landscape and decipher the evidence, the *Wild Things* series has its own expert plant detectives on hand – top botanist Dr Trevor Dines and lichenologist Sally Eaton, as well as garden designer Chris Myers. The *Wild Things* team likes nothing more than being outside and up to their knees and eyes in the stuff that grows, creeps and crawls through our countryside. If it's growing, they know where to find it; when it's not where it should be, they can explain why.

Together, the team provides specialist knowledge and experience of the landscapes around us. As they embark on a cross-country journey around the British Isles, they'll reveal unexpected stories and surprising facts. Through the tales of individual species, such as our native bluebells (*Hyacinthoides non-scripta*) and common poppies (*Papaver rhoeas*), it'll become clear that plants can achieve much more than we might have imagined (see chapters 2 and 6). Some, such as archaeophytes (ancient plants), provide living links with our distant history, dating back to the Stone Age, *c*.4000–2500 BC (see p.210); other species, including lichens, might help alert us to changes in the atmosphere, such as a rise in pollution levels (see pp.108–9).

For our plant detectives, each species throws up intriguing puzzles, such as the amazing ability of juniper (*Juniperus communis*) to survive extreme cold; the unusual taste for salt displayed by Danish scurvygrass (*Cochlearia danica*); or the recent sudden spread of prickly lettuce (*Lactuca serriola*). The conundrums raised by plants are like detective mysteries that need to be unravelled; and our very own plant sleuths, the *Wild Things* team, are hot on the case, solving different puzzles in each chapter. Why, for instance, does alpine penny-cress (*Noccaea caerulescens*) grow near mines? How and why do waterbears change shape under stress? What's prompting mossy stonecrop (*Crassula tillaea*) to spread north? To find out, turn to chapters 1 and 2. In the television series, too, the *Wild Things* team tackle different and intriguing plant mysteries during each episode.

A journey without end

With its illuminating stories, investigative experiments and vibrant photographs, *The Wild Things Guide* will help you to read the landscape as never before, enabling you to make bigger, broader connections between the birds and the bees, the plants and the animals.

Chapter 1 explains in more detail how the BSBI's natural history project came to life and how to unpack the clues buried in the distribution maps, which in turn can crucially help to change the way in which we view the countryside. Across the following six chapters, the *Wild Things* team investigate some of the British Isles' key habitats to see how plant life across the landscape is changing – moving, spreading and, sometimes, disappearing. Habitats with which we're all familiar, such as woodlands and mountains, farmlands and gardens, will be explored alongside

BELOW *A chaffinch perches on a lichen-covered branch. As lichens are highly sensitive to the quality of air that they absorb from the atmosphere, they can often serve as pollutant indicators.*

BOTTOM *The rare mountain avens (*Dryas octopetala*) is an arctic-alpine plant now found on our highest summits.*

Yellow flag iris (Iris pseudacorus) and white hemlock water-dropwort (Oenanthe crocata) line the edge of the Grand Western Canal in Devon, southwest England. Transport networks, such as canals, often create long stretches of new habitat along which wild things can move through the countryside.

more unusual homes, such as roadside verges and canal towpaths. Even in the better-known habitats, the team will reveal recent discoveries about wild plants and why some are changing on the quiet. In chapter 2, which explores our woodlands, you'll hear the extraordinary tale of the mysterious ghost orchid (*Epipogium aphyllum*) that lives almost entirely underground; you'll learn how to recognize centuries-old woodlands; discover why certain fungi glow in the dark and why our iconic bluebell dells are now under threat.

Chapter 3 investigates what's growing in the new wild spaces created by our road, rail and canal networks. Our transport system might sound like an unpromising starting point, but the soft verges and hard shoulders of our motorways have become some of the British Isles' best nature reserves. On the edges of our modern highways, along our railroads, canals and towpaths, unexpected pockets of abundant plant life flourishes, having somehow managed to travel hundreds of miles around the country to put down roots in new man-made homes.

In chapter 4, the team explore our uplands and mountains, where they discover the delights of juniper berries – the main ingredient in gin – and trace the cause of their decline, while also investigating our stunning hanging gardens, precious arctic-alpines and summit lichens which, amazingly, thrive on cold, bare mountain tops.

Chapter 5, featuring our farmlands, shows how modern agriculture has changed the shape and colour of the landscape. You'll hear some sobering tales about our once familiar cornfield flowers and ancient hay meadows; master the art of telling a meadow's age just from its buttercup petals; and discover why some poppy fields are no longer a common sight, while others are on the increase.

In chapter 6, on garden plants, the *Wild Things* team take a long hard look at the many exotic non-native plants that we've cultivated in our gardens, from where they've escaped into the wild, adding colour and variety to the landscape, but also affecting our countryside and urban wild spaces in countless unexpected ways.

Revealing discoveries

Alongside the stories of individual plants, investigative strands throughout the book unfold the key stages of various laboratory and field experiments that were carried out during the making of the television series. Each experiment answers an intriguing question, such as why the scent of bluebells is so refreshing or how certain roadside plants have learnt to hitch a ride on the backdraft of our fast cars (see pp.68–9, 102–3).

Together, the illuminating distribution maps, inquiring experiments and compelling plant trails produce a vibrant snapshot of the richness of the British Isles' natural world. By the end of their journey, the *Wild Things* team will have pieced together the clues picked up along the way, and connected the disparate strands of each story. They'll analyse the findings revealed by the latest maps and evidence to assess the implications for wildlife as a whole. In the light of their discoveries, the team will review modern conservation, question whether we're getting things right and see what future developments we can anticipate.

The Wild Things Guide opens an inviting window onto the natural world of wild plants and other wildlife. Offering a view from the grassroots up, it highlights unexpected ways in which you can reconnect with your own natural backyard. You can be sure that, by the time you've reached the end of this book, you'll never look at the great outdoors in quite the same way again.

CLARE JONES, TV PRODUCER, *WILD THINGS*

Yellow meadow buttercups (Ranunculus acris) flourish in North Tyne Valley, Northumberland, where pastures are often traditionally managed to ensure that wildflower seeds are shed before the grass is cut for hay each year.

THE *WILD THINGS* TEAM

Sally Eaton

LICHENOLOGIST • ECOLOGIST • HAND-LENS HOLDER

Saving up for a secondhand microscope was the turning point in Sally's life. At the age of just thirteen, a whole new world suddenly opened up to her. Before long, this budding ecologist was dissecting flowers and pulling the wings off dead flies to study them. Things haven't changed much since then.

Growing up in the middle of nowhere in an old farmhouse in the Forest of Bowland in deepest, darkest Lancashire, northwest England, certainly helped cement Sally's love of the great outdoors and the wild things. She spent her days roaming the hills and woods, foraging for living things and bringing home anything that she could find.

From the early days of that first microscope, there was always some experiment going on in her bedroom, whether she was sprinkling sugar on the carpet to encourage flies to lay eggs, or leaving a glass of milk on the window ledge in the excited hope of seeing fungi grow on its surface. There was even one occasion when her mum found a clutch of ducks' eggs that Sally was trying to hatch in the airing cupboard; another time, she discovered an opened tin of dog food that Sally was feeding to her tadpoles under the bed.

It was Gerald Durrell's book, *The Amateur Naturalist* (1983), that further fuelled Sally's desire to explore and experiment. By the age of sixteen, she and a friend had hatched a plan to visit India. She worked in a cafe to save the money for the expedition, which really opened her eyes to the world's diversity, both natural and cultural, and made her eager to explore even more.

After completing her schooling, she eventually left the safe folds of the Forest of Bowland and headed north to the big smoke of Edinburgh in Scotland to study for

Sally gets just as excited exploring the tiny landscapes of lichens and mosses (above) as she does investigating the natural wonders of the wider countryside (top).

a degree in ecology. Despite falling in love with the city, four years later she was off again, this time to join a research trip to Kalimantan, the Indonesian part of the island of Borneo. Here she worked in a tropical swamp forest mapping the effects that illegal logging has had on the rainforest. A slightly more nine-to-five job as an ecological consultant for an international engineering firm eventually followed, but Sally didn't stay put in one place for too long.

The island of Madagascar in the Indian Ocean was her next stop, where she took up a new position as a research scientist. Here she spent a year living in a tent and filled her days with chasing snakes, catching geckoes, watching lemurs and, most excitingly of all, collecting and recording all the weird and wonderful plants in the forest. There were flowers, fruits and trees that she had never seen before. It was the first place where she 'didn't have a clue what anything was', and loved it.

After a nasty snake bite, though, she returned to the relative safety of home and decided to do something about her new-found passion for plants. She gained a scholarship position on a Masters course in plant taxonomy and biodiversity at the Royal Botanic Garden Edinburgh in Scotland. Here she learned how to identify things, how plants evolved and how they came to grow where we see them today. But the most fascinating discovery of all during that year was the world of lichens, as Sally recalls:

This miniature world had been under my feet quite literally my whole life, but I'd never pointed my hand-lens in the right direction to notice it. Tree bark soon became a mountainous landscape of peaks and troughs, each harbouring secret delights; and pebbles and rocks became huge boulders that I could spend hours examining.

Today Sally works as a research assistant at the Royal Botanic Garden Edinburgh, where she studies the diversity of lichens and bryophytes in Scotland's woodlands. She is also chair of the Education and Promotions Committee of the British Lichen Society and a trustee of the Species Recovery Trust. So those very small and once unseen bits of life now occupy much of Sally's working day and spare time. It turns out that £15 for that first microscope was very well spent.

Sally surveys Salisbury Plain in Wiltshire, southern England, searching for the hidden wonders that lie beneath our feet.

CHAPTER ONE

WHERE THE WILD THINGS GROW

The British Isles has quite possibly the most fully recorded and best understood plant life in the world. At least 7,544 different species have been discovered growing in the wild and nearly 20 million individual plants, mosses and lichens have been recorded and verified.

This comprehensive census of wild things, organized by various botanical societies, has been painstakingly gathered over the last fifty years from a mass of modern and historical evidence (see pp.12–13, 27–8). One of the most ambitious projects ever undertaken in natural history, it involves the dedicated efforts of teams of amateur enthusiasts and expert naturalists who go out into the field every year to record and report on plant life across the country. The fruits of their labour first appeared fifty years ago in the ground-breaking *Atlas of the British Flora* (1962), a collection of plant distribution maps, showing where all plants growing in the wild had been found throughout the British Isles.

Today, the work continues as we expand one of the most exhaustive surveys of wild plants ever attempted. The detailed recording of all species across the British Isles carries on quietly behind the scenes as dedicated plant lovers continue to amass and update evidence (see p.27).

*PREVIOUS PAGE Even the smallest patch of land can be home to some wonderfully exuberant wild things, such as these oxeye daisies (*Leucanthemum vulgare*), a common sight on roadside verges and in wildflower meadows.*

BELOW Lichenologist Sally Eaton searches for rare lichens in the chalk grassland of Salisbury Plain in Wiltshire, southern England.

As a result of the continuous monitoring up and down the country, we can now periodically gather all the information in the census together, allowing us to investigate and evaluate any changes over a specific time span. By comparing the latest maps for a particular plant today with the original data published in the 1962 *Atlas*, we can clearly see what's been going on in the wild over the past fifty years and work out exactly which plants have been spreading across the country and which ones might be shrinking from our towns and cities, as well as our countryside.

As plants form the fundamental building blocks of most ecosystems, this huge body of evidence can now be used as a touchstone against which to gauge just how healthy our green and pleasant land really is. If certain plants are declining, for instance, what effect will their disappearance have on other wild things that depend on them for food and shelter? Equally, if new arrivals from abroad are moving in unnoticed, how will they affect the balance of nature all around us? Will the newcomers push out the natives that have been with us for centuries? If so, does it matter?

The maps provide some crucial answers. If we can learn to spot the clues buried in the evidence and interpret the patterns revealed in the *Atlas*, we should be able to discover why so many plants are altering at such a dramatic rate across our landscape. For the first time ever in our history, we can now monitor and analyse the constant flux in nature throughout the British Isles. Because this census of wild things covers such a vast expanse and spans more than half a century, it allows us to really assess the scale of change, which often goes unnoticed.

Botanist Dr Trevor Dines tracks down Himalayan balsam in the fields around the village of Llanrug, North Wales, to monitor the rapid spread of this non-native newcomer (see pp.180–2).

SQUARING UP TO NATURE

Cast your eye over any of the plant maps in this book. What do you see? In almost every case, you'll immediately detect a distinctive pattern of dots – sprinkled, spattered or sprawled across the outline of the British Isles. For plant detectives, these infinitely varied patterns provide a primary source of evidence, the 'white line' taped around 'the body' in a sleuth mystery. The little dots on the plant maps provide the first clues on the whereabouts and movements of the wild things in our towns, cities and the countryside around us. When correctly read and interpreted, these dotted distribution

ABOVE All standard Ordnance Survey (OS) maps in the British Isles show a 10km-square (hectad) grid, seen here with a magnetic compass. Map-reading and navigating are essential skills for plant detectives out in the field.

RIGHT The map shows Britain and Ireland divided into a regular grid of 10km squares (hectads). For the purposes of surveying our wild things, naturalists compile a complete list of every plant growing within each hectad, which can encompass well over 700 species in some places.

THE 10KM-SQUARE GRID
DIVIDING THE BRITISH ISLES
INTO 3,859 10KM SQUARES
(HECTADS)

maps can help us to spot and assess vital shifts in the patterns of nature. The pictures built up by these plant maps are quite astonishing. So what exactly do the dots tell us?

Each dot represents a hectad (10km square) of land, teeming with plant life. You might wonder why a hectad exactly, rather than something more expansive or more detailed? The hectad grid forms the basis of the British Ordnance Survey (OS) mapping system, which was first developed in 1936. Similar grids were then produced for Ireland and the Channel Islands, dividing the whole of Britain and Ireland into 3,859 10km squares. The hectad grid provides a system that has now become constant and universal.

Detectives on the trail

How exactly is the mass of evidence gathered for the plant distribution maps? It's essentially down to an army of volunteer plant detectives and their appetite for searching, naming and cataloguing wild things. All the records that they collect on the whereabouts of our wild plants are then filtered through the Botanical Society of the British Isles (BSBI). This charity traces its origins back to 1836, when it was founded as the Botanical Society of London.

Today, there are almost 3,000 BSBI volunteer plant detectives, who come from all walks of life – from dentists and postmen, to dinner ladies. They are almost always self-taught – expert amateurs in the best tradition of British naturalists. They spend their spare time searching the length and breadth of all parts of the British Isles. Wind or rain, they climb mountains, wade in muddy bogs and scale rocky sea cliffs carrying out their investigations, hunting for new plants and checking up on the old familiar ones too.

Out in the field, plant detectives Trevor Dines (top), Sally Eaton (below left) and Chris Myers (below right) gather and inspect evidence on species growing in the wild.

It's the sheer enjoyment of discovery that motivates many to get out and explore their local patch, whether it's a city or village, a park or the open countryside. There's a certain thrill in chancing upon the unexpected, discovering new arrivals; and it's satisfying to renew old botanical acquaintances that you've not seen growing in the wild for years. Unlike many other wild things, plants can be touched, smelled and tasted; you can revisit them each year and build up a relationship with them over time.

Our volunteer plant detectives are the powerhouse of the BSBI and other botanical societies, such as the British Lichen Society and the Bryological Society (see pp.50–1). Without them, we'd have much less knowledge about how our natural world works.

Ground-breaking maps

For every dot on a plant map, someone has gone out to investigate a particular hectad of British or Irish soil and recorded all the different plants growing there. Each species found on the ground is then given just one dot on the map, regardless of how many plants might actually be growing in that one hectad. It's only when all the dots have been plotted that a broader picture emerges and the whole story starts to unfold.

The OS hectad grid was first used in a natural history atlas in 1962 when the landmark *Atlas of the British Flora* was published (see p.24). The OS system proved to be an excellent way of listing and plotting on a national scale the exact location of wild things. The method has since been used to map other forms of wildlife including birds, bugs and butterflies (see pp.48–9). Today, the OS system is counted as the standard model for creating such distribution maps but, back in 1962, the *Atlas* generated an exciting new interest in biogeography – the study of why things grow and live where they do.

Tracing lost tracks

To track down plants that might have disappeared, such as downy hemp-nettle (*Galeopsis segetum*), for which there is an ongoing search, plant detectives often investigate old historical records, including sketch maps and herbaria (collections of pressed plants). Although original sketch plans can look rather like a pirate's treasure map, with an 'X' marking the buried hoard, they can be surprisingly reliable, sometimes leading us along the exact route taken by naturalists decades, maybe centuries ago, as in the case of spreading bellflower (*Campanula patula*). After faithfully following the old trail, a quick rummage around with the dog revealed the exact spot where the plant had previously been seen in 1868. Remarkably there it was in 2003, still growing where it had last been recorded 135 years ago.

Herbaria provide other essential clues. In these wonderful collections of pressed plants, sometimes 300 years old, samples have been carefully catalogued by date, location and recorder. Very old specimens can show us what grew where in the past. As well as providing direct historical records of species that can be plotted on the plant maps, herbaria also hint at what could still be around. Dune gentian (*Gentianella uliginosa*), for instance, was rediscovered at Braunton Burrows, Devon, after herbarium specimens from 1849 were unearthed at the British Museum, prompting a search for the lost plant.

Labelled jars of dried and preserved medicinal herbs in the herbarium at the Royal Botanical Gardens in Kew, Surrey, southeast England. The largest herbarium in the world, it contains over 5 million plant specimens.

Today, the Global Positioning System (GPS) and electronic aerial photographs are revolutionizing our detective work, allowing us to pin down the position of plants more precisely than ever before. If you can't find ciliate strap lichen (*Heterodermia leucomela*) after searching for hours and failing to spot it, power up the GPS, follow the co-ordinates and look down at your feet – there it is, a tiny patch just 3cm across!

INSPECTING THE EVIDENCE

Once the evidence has been gathered by the plant detectives, various bodies, including the Botanical Society of the British Isles, the Biological Records Centre and the National Biodiversity Network, play a crucial role in collating and analysing the data amassed.

As a stream of records is constantly flowing in from the detectives in the field, it helps to set deadlines for collating and publishing the

Hand-held Global Positioning System (GPS) devices allow botanists to make highly accurate grid references and pinpoint the exact location of plants that have been recorded in the past.

WHEN IS A PLANT WILD?

When we talk about plants being found 'in the wild', we usually mean that they're growing outside our gardens without having been deliberately planted. Often, though, garden plants can 'escape over the garden wall' into the wild and spread by themselves, in which case they're described as having become 'naturalized'. For the ongoing BSBI survey on wild species (see pp.24–7), if plants are found quite literally at the base of a garden wall, they tend to be discounted, since they're still too close to the garden. If they've reached the other side of the road, though, or started spreading down the verge or high street, then they're viewed as wild (right).

What of native species that develop in a garden without having been planted (see p.33)? All natives that grow by themselves, even in a garden, are regarded as wild things and included in the BSBI survey of wild plants. Gardeners, though, tend to use another term for them – weeds.

After a long trek to a secret destination, Trevor and Chris discover a clump of lady's-slipper orchid, one of the rarest flowers in the British Isles. For every plant found in the wild, a dot is plotted on the distribution maps for the species. Even rarities are mapped, although the exact location of the rarest, such as the orchid here, remains confidential.

data. At set points in time, at present around every fifty years, the evidence is published in a new edition of the *Atlas of the British Flora* (now the *Atlas of the British and Irish Flora*). A publication deadline prompts a concerted effort to gather in all the records to date and plot them on maps. The series of maps generated as a result provides an illuminating snapshot of emerging trends across the British Isles, rather like taking a stock check of our wild things.

The first target deadline for publication was set in 1962, when data collected since the 1950s were plotted on the maps and formed the basis of the original *Atlas of the British Flora* (1962). A sequel was scheduled for 2002, which meant revisiting all areas of the British Isles to check if the same plants remained where they'd been before and to discover whether new plants were now growing in unexpected places.

From year to year, more records come flowing in, but we have to wait for a reasonable period, at least ten years, before assessing whether a particular pattern of distribution is actually changing or whether it's just a temporary fluctuation. Today, with at least fifty years' worth of evidence gathered from the wild in the British Isles, we are now in a unique position to be able to conduct a more rigorous scientific assessment of these maps. By now, we have enough information to make sense of the incredible scale of change that has taken place throughout the country.

UNLOCKING THE CLUES

The distribution maps often throw up a conundrum that needs to be solved, such as the sudden spread, or equally abrupt decline, of a species (see pp.34–6). If the clues within the maps can be accurately interpreted, they can often help solve the mystery of why a plant might be on the march, falling by the wayside or moving into new quarters.

The case of the plant next door

The clues can sometimes be quite clear – a map plastered in dots, for instance, indicates a common plant, such as ribwort plantain (*Plantago lanceolata*). Its distribution pattern (below) is absolutely solid, with more dots packed into the outline of the British Isles than in any other case, so it's no surprise to learn that it is the most widespread plant in the country. In fact, we now have records of ribwort plantain growing in every single hectad of the grid.

Ribwort plantain (inset) is remarkably tough and able to tolerate a huge range of ecological conditions. As it can grow almost anywhere, it is recorded from every single hectad in the British Isles. The apparently open square seen on the map east of Edinburgh (centre top) is actually open sea.

RIBWORT PLANTAIN
PLANTAGO LANCEOLATA

TODAY

A map this smothered in dots tells us that ribwort plantain can tolerate a huge range of conditions, whether wet or dry, sunny or shady, with poor or nutrient-rich soil – in effect, it has a high ecological tolerance and can grow absolutely anywhere. Ribwort plantain flourishes in our towns and cities as well as in the countryside, from Land's End in Cornwall, southwest England, to John o'Groats in northern Scotland. It is so common, in fact, that it tends to be ignored. If you can't quite place it, think back to your childhood – you might have played a game with the plant where you picked the stems and flicked the flower heads at your playmates.

The case of the exclusive lily

A single dot on the plant map for Radnor lily (inset top) spells out the precious rarity of this fabled Welsh flower, which grows only on Stanner Rocks in Powys, mid Wales (inset bottom).

Other maps graphically illustrate the extraordinary rarity of a plant. A species such as Radnor lily (*Gagea bohemica*), for instance, has only ever been found growing in one hectad in Powys, mid Wales (below). The delicate yellow lily is undoubtedly one of our rarest plants, although it is not the only species represented by just one dot on the national distribution maps. Other comparable rarities include Suffolk lungwort (*Pulmonaria obscura)* and wood calamint (*Clinopodium*

RADNOR LILY
GAGEA BOHEMICA

TODAY

menthifolium). In the case of Radnor lily, we might wonder what's so special about the one hectad where it thrives? Investigation reveals that the dot on the map marks Stanner Rocks, a hill where the oldest outcrops in southern Britain come to the surface. Over 711 million years old, today's Stanner Rocks first arose from a fragment of Avalonia, a micro-continent that split away from Gondwanaland, the very earliest landmass on earth. The surviving igneous granites and gabbros have a strange chemistry, unlike that of any other stone in the British Isles. Something in their chemical make-up has enabled the thin, dry soils that cover the hill at Stanner Rocks to support a unique collection of plants, including Radnor lily, found nowhere else in the British Isles.

SPOTTING UPCOMING TRENDS

Looking at the maps as a whole can reveal broader trends. One pattern that clearly emerges is that many, at least half of the 4,111 plants mapped in the latest *Atlas* are on the increase, including both pervasive natives, such as common nettle (*Urtica dioica*), and fast-spreading newcomers, such as buddleja (*Buddleia davidii*) (see pp.35–6).

NATIVES *VERSUS* NON-NATIVES

At the end of the last Ice Age, around 10,000 years ago, what are now the British Isles were still connected to the European mainland, so plants could spread freely across the landmass moving north and west in the wake of the retreating ice sheets.

As the ice melted and sea levels rose, however, the English Channel filled with water, and the British Isles took shape. Now cut off by water, mainland plants could no longer make their way across to the British Isles. The ones that had arrived under their own steam before the Channel flooded became known as our 'native' species, such as selfheal (*Prunella vulgaris*) (above left). Later, with the invention of boats and the development of trade in ancient times, mainland plants made the crossing again.

Over time, a rich variety of exotic species arrived from abroad on the backs of traders, explorers and gardeners. We brought in plants to provide food, drink and medicine; for their timber, fibres and dyes; for flowers to grow and enjoy. Many of the newcomers, or 'non-natives', such as Himalayan balsam (*Impatiens glandulifera*) (above right) have since escaped from gardens and found their way into the wild (see p.29).

At the same time, alarmingly, many of the distribution maps show a decline in some icons of our countryside, especially among the plants associated with our farmland, arable fields and meadows, such as corn marigold (*Chrysanthemum segetum*) and corn buttercup (*Ranunculus arvensis*) (below). Many would have been familiar sights in our landscape fifty years ago, yet within a lifetime, something has occurred that has had a huge effect on some of our most common flowers.

The case of the vanishing buttercup

Corn buttercup (*Ranunculus arvensis*) is a classic example of a declining flower. Its pattern of dots has shrunk quite rapidly in a matter of years. Just take a look at the paired maps for the plant (below). The one on the left shows where the buttercup had been recorded in the British Isles up to the year 2000, while the map on its right reveals where the plant has been found since 2000. Clearly, there has been a catastrophic decline over a very short period, demonstrated by a shrinking pattern of dots since 2000. Something has happened on a huge scale for the buttercup to vanish from our countryside. It's only by analysing these distribution maps across

ABOVE *Corn buttercup grows alongside crops, such as wheat and barley.*

BELOW *The maps reveal that since 2000 corn buttercup has all but disappeared.*

CORN BUTTERCUP
RANUNCULUS ARVENSIS

BEFORE
2000

TODAY

a specific time span that we can hope to monitor and catch such important changes. Without the maps, the plant's decline might have passed unnoticed. To see exactly why corn buttercup has been disappearing, read chapter 6.

The case of the pushy new bush

Other familiar plants are on the increase according to the latest plant maps, which show a rise in non-natives especially, such as the popular garden plant buddleja (*Buddleia davidii*). The two distribution maps for the species (below) illustrate a dramatic change in the pattern of its spread in the wild since 1962. While the map on the left reveals where buddleja had grown until 1962, the one on the right indicates where it has since been found until the present time. Its startling growth over the last fifty years immediately raises some burning questions: how on earth could such a massive increase have occurred? What precipitated the plant's rapid expansion and what effect has it had on other plants and wild things in the surrounding countryside? To unravel the buddleja story, turn to chapter 5.

BELOW Buddleja, commonly known as the butterfly bush, attracts many butterflies, such as this brimstone.

BOTTOM The remarkable spread of buddleja across Britain and Ireland since 1962 is clearly illustrated by the paired distribution maps for the plant.

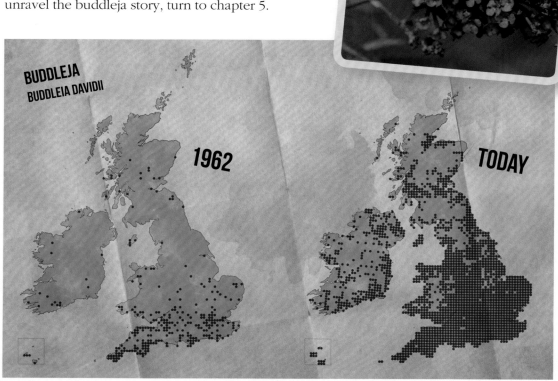

BUDDLEJA
BUDDLEIA DAVIDII

1962

TODAY

ABOVE *Each green speck is a plant of least duckweed.*

BELOW *Ponds populated by least duckweed are soon covered by a green carpet of leaf-like plants, often spread by water fowl.*

The case of the non-stop duckweed

Another newcomer on the move, least duckweed (*Lemna minuta*) is spreading at top speed. Just a quick glance at the paired maps for the plant (opposite) will reveal a dramatic increase in its distribution since it was first discovered growing in the wild in the British Isles in 1977. The dramatic change shown over the past thirty-five years indicates that this is a plant whose main mission in life is to get around and find its way into new places where it can grow and multiply rapidly. Although currently one of the fastest-spreading plants in the British Isles, least duckweed is also one of the smallest, just 2.5mm long. Living on the surface of ponds, lakes and canals, it produces tiny floating, leaf-like bodies that split off from each other and can double in number every two days. Carried around from pond to pond on the bodies of ducks, geese, swans and other water birds, these tiny individual plants quickly spread, covering the surface of the water in a fine, green carpet (below). It's definitely an unwelcome plant if you find it growing in your pond.

LEAST DUCKWEED
LEMNA MINUTA

1977

TODAY

INVESTIGATING THE LAY OF THE LAND

To get the most out of the plant distribution maps, we should also remember to take a broader view and look at where different species are growing from a more geographical perspective. Just by analysing exactly where a particular plant thrives – whether in the warm south or cool north – we can deduce quite a lot.

For the first clue – look south

Take a plant like black bryony (*Tamus communis*). The map for its distribution (overleaf) reveals an obvious north–south divide. It's as if a line has been drawn from Cumbria in northwest England across to Newcastle-upon-Tyne in northeast England. North of this line, the plant simply vanishes. South of this divide and it seems fairly widespread, apart from areas in the Pennines and the Welsh Mountains in western Britain. Clearly, black bryony doesn't seem too fussy, just so long as it stays south of the divide. What is it north of Cumbria that the plant cannot tolerate? As a climber closely related to tropical yams (*Dioscorea* sp.), black bryony needs warmth and a long summer. Its bright red berries take at least 100 days – a good three months – to

The startling spread of least duckweed from southeast England since its discovery in the wild in 1977 is clearly captured in the plant's distribution maps here. For such fast-moving species, the maps are always changing: in another fifty years we'd expect the plant to have reached most of southern Britain and to be heading north and west.

BLACK BRYONY
TAMUS COMMUNIS

TODAY

ABOVE The map for black bryony (insets) shows a remarkable cut-off just north of Cumbria, beyond which the plant simply doesn't grow. From its distribution map, we can clearly see that black bryony is a warmth-loving southern species.

RIGHT Blackberries (Rubus fruticosus) and the red berries of black bryony ripen in the late summer sunshine. Although black bryony berries are highly poisonous, blackberries, of course, are a popular edible fruit used in puddings and jams.

CHICKWEED WINTERGREEN
TRIENTALIS EUROPAEA

TODAY

ripen fully. The seed then needs a full six months' winter dormancy followed by precise spring temperatures to stimulate germination. Clearly, black bryony is fussy about warmth and won't grow where the average July temperatures fail to rise above 15°C – in fact, the cut-off line on the map above Cumbria indicates almost exactly where the average temperature remains below 15°C in July.

Now look north

In complete contrast, here's a cool customer confined to the coldest parts of the British Isles. Chickweed wintergreen (*Trientalis europaea*) needs low temperatures to survive. In fact, it's limited to areas where average July temperatures don't rise above 15.6°C. It grows best when the temperature remains between 11 and 18°C, above which it cannot fix carbon dioxide from the atmosphere, causing growth to slow right down and the plant to struggle. Wherever summer temperatures rise, outside Scotland and northern England, this species simply can't grow.

Chickweed wintergreen (inset), a northern plant of deciduous woodlands, thrives on acidic soil. As revealed by its distribution map, it grows only in the coldest parts of the British Isles where summers remain cool. In the heat, its metabolism shuts down and the plant just stops growing.

SPRING SQUILL
SCILLA VERNA

TODAY

Next, go west

Hugging the coast as if the edge of the map's been dipped in chocolate, spring squill (*Scilla verna*) really hates the cold. The dots on its distribution map show that it rarely grows more than a few miles inland from western coasts, where the Gulf Stream currents keep the winters warm and wet. Average February temperatures here generally remain above 5 or 6°C. In these conditions, spring squill starts growth in late winter, flowers in early spring and disappears below ground by summer. Species that only flourish in this type of warm, moist maritime climate are what's called 'hyperoceanic'. Spring squill displays exactly the same preferences wherever it grows along the Atlantic Arc, which runs around the western coasts of Portugal, Spain, France, the British Isles and on up to the Faroe Islands and Norway. Many other hyperoceanic plants, such as portland spurge (*Euphorbia portlandica*) and rock sea-spurrey (*Spergularia rupicola*), show a similar coast-hugging pattern of distribution.

REVEALING THE NATURE OF NATURE

Although a plant's character and preferences can help explain why it grows where it does – whether in the cool north or warmer south – nothing remains constant or entirely predictable, as plants don't live in isolation but as part of a dynamic web of life, including ourselves. Looking at the clues on the maps from wider perspectives – biogeographical, geological and social – can highlight the extraordinary connections between living things and explain some puzzling shifts in distribution. Take the effect of our own presence: our towns, cities and countryside abound in change and, over the centuries, our actions and activities have affected the landscape. We've farmed the land differently, built cities, factories and transport networks, and pumped chemicals into our atmosphere that rain down upon everything. At the same time, nature has undergone its own fluctuations, including global shifts in climate.

Whether natural or man-made, the dynamics of change constantly impinge on wild things and where they grow. As plants aren't rooted to the spot, sooner or later they'll react to changes in their environment and spread out to grasp fresh opportunities, or shrink back when conditions turn bad. The clues lie in the plant maps – in the pattern of the dots and the pictures they paint. Each map reflects the character of a plant and the history of our countryside. We just have to see the connections.

Reflecting the nature of the land, two moisture-loving plants, purple loosestrife (Lythrum salicaria) and frothy white meadowsweet (Filipendula ulmaria), flourish on a damp, ungrazed patch beside the coast at Mile Long Beach on the Isle of Jura, Scotland.

MAKING THE CONNECTIONS

Just look around at almost any habitat, whether grasslands or woodlands, heathlands or hedgerows, and you'll quickly realize that they're all constructed from specific vegetation that defines their character. Quite simply, plants form the basic building blocks of many habitats, while also providing essential food and shelter for the myriad other wild things that flourish alongside them (see opposite). The connection is clear – if we look after the plants, all our other wild things have a much better chance of survival.

In light of the keystone role played by plants in any particular habitat, we don't always need to look far to discover why other wild things, such as certain birds, butterflies and bees, might have increased or decreased. Just by reading the clues in the *Atlas* and comparing the distribution maps of different species, we can make valid connections. The recent decline in bees, for instance, is linked to the loss of grassland wildflowers that traditionally provided them with a variety of pollen and nectar (see chapter 6). A similar drop in farmland birds is connected to the decrease in cornfield flowers, which customarily supplied birds with a rich mix of seed. Connections even closer to home, literally beneath our feet, can also emerge, as the next cases reveal.

Suspended between stems of grass, a spider's cobweb sparkles in the sunrise over a water-meadow near Stockbridge, Hampshire, southern England. These exceptional meadows are home to more than 100 species of plants that support at least 200 different types of insects, snails, worms and spiders.

What is a plant?

From towering pines to tiny speedwells, green plants include the familiar trees, bushes, fruits, vegetables, flowers and herbs that we see all around us. Many have played a central role in our lives: clothing, feeding, sheltering and, sometimes, healing us. We've clambered into their branches for fruit; picked their flowers for our loved ones; and enjoyed a reviving tea from their leaves, or a refreshing gin from their berries (see p.131).

Natural diversity

Plants are extraordinarily varied, ranging from the soaring giants of the forest, up to 60m tall, to the smallest mosses, just 1mm long. Some species live for thousands of years, such as yew (*Taxus baccata*), while herbaceous plants, such as poppies (*Papaver rhoeas*) complete their life-cycle in just one year. The rich diversity of plants reflects their ability to thrive in amazingly varied conditions, whether wet or dry, sunny or shady, acidic or alkaline.

The so-called higher plants, such as trees, shrubs and flowers, have roots, stems and leaves composed of vascular tissues, which transport water and nutrients around the plant. By contrast, small, low-growing plants, such as liverworts and mosses (the bryophytes), lack vascular tissues, true stems, leaves or roots, but are anchored to the ground by rhizoids. Algae (*protista*) and fungi (*fungi*) have some plant-like characteristics, although they are not really regarded as true plants (see p.45).

The next generation

Plant reproduction can be equally varied. Trees, shrubs and flowering plants all reproduce by spreading seed, whether borne by wind, water or animals (see p.116). Flowering plants develop wonderfully varied colours and scents to attract pollinating insects (see p.66), while non-flowering

The short-lived common poppy (above) flourishes in crop fields, flowering, dying and shedding its seeds within a year, while the gnarled and ancient oaks in Horner Wood, Somerset (top), endure for hundreds of years.

plants, such as conifers, produce wind-borne, seed-bearing cones instead (see p.143). Ferns, horsetails and clubmosses, by contrast, generate spores rather than seed (see p.79).

The green in greenery

Despite their diversity, all green plants have one thing in common – green chlorophyll, which is the incredible substance used in photosynthesis to capture energy from sunlight with which to create glucose sugar from nothing more than water and carbon dioxide. The sugar produced fuels the plant, as well as sustaining many wild things on the planet, while the oxygen released as a by-product of photosynthesis also supports the majority of life on earth. Basically, green plants provide both the fuel and oxygen needed for almost all other life – they are, quite literally, the lungs and powerhouse of the planet.

One plant's meat is another's poison

To the vast majority of plants, heavy metals such as lead and zinc are utterly poisonous, but a dozen or so flowering species and quite a few lichens and mosses have developed a taste for them.

Alpine penny-cress (*Noccaea caerulescens*), also called leadwort, positively flourishes on sites where underlying lead- and zinc-rich rocks have come to the surface, either naturally or through mining and its left-over slag heaps, laden with poisonous metals. Indeed, leadwort was once used by miners as a species indicator, marking the presence of lead just below the surface of the ground where it grew. Plants that have built up a tolerance to heavy metals actively take up the poisons and store them in their tissues as a defence against certain diseases and herbivores.

Several species of lichen, too, such as the silver-grey coral lichen (*Stereocaulon vesuvianum*), flourish in sites rich in toxic heavy metals, including lead and zinc.

The distribution map for alpine penny-cress (inset top) accurately reveals where lead- and zinc-rich rocks come to the surface. The pattern of dots clearly picks out the lead mines of the Yorkshire Dales and Pennines (inset bottom) in northern England.

ALPINE PENNY-CRESS
NOCCAEA CAERULESCENS

TODAY

What is a lichen?

A lichen is not a species; it is not an organism; it is not a plant; and it is not an animal. What on earth is it, then? A lichen is a way of life! It is made up of at least two species living in a 'symbiotic' relationship whereby both partners benefit.

The lichen way

Together the two partners form a perfectly balanced capsule that needs little more than the surrounding atmosphere for its survival. One of the partners is almost always a type of fungus called an ascomycete. Unlike green plants, fungi cannot use energy from sunlight to produce their own food by photosynthesis (see p.43). Instead, if they're not in a lichen partnership, fungi survive either by eating live things or by living off dead things, or alternatively by exchanging nutrients with other living things.

The fungus within a lichen home, however, acquires food by living with a food-producing partner – usually a single-celled green algae, though sometimes a blue-green bacteria – which can produce sugars by photosynthesis. The fungus in its turn supplies the algae with water and other nutrients gathered from the atmosphere, as well as protecting it from harsh sunlight, the risk of drying out and bacterial or herbivorous attack.

The lichen home

Together, the partners create the crusty, leafy or shrubby lichen structures often seen on rocks, walls and trees. Though the form and variety of species present within lichens can vary enormously, the basic lichen shape is usually sandwich-like, with a top layer of protective fungus; a middle layer of food-producing algae; and a loose lower layer of fungus that stores water and allows air to circulate. Sometimes an additional base fungal layer attaches the lichen to rock, bark or soil.

By growing together, the partners in a lichen capsule can flourish in inhospitable places where they might not otherwise survive alone, such as the Namib Desert, southern Africa (above), carpeted with fields of Teloschistes capensis; or on bare rock face (top), plastered with the map lichen.

Mutual benefits

Why do fungi and algae come together in this way to live the lichen lifestyle? Without the protection of a fungus, algae are usually confined to damp places, as they dry out easily. Safe within a fungus, though, they're freer to thrive in more varied homes. Without the algae, the fungus would be confined to living only where it could find food, such as near dead matter. By carrying a food factory around with it, the fungus, like the algae, can be much freer in its choice of home.

Needing little more than each other to survive and taking on a variety of forms, the partners within a lichen are able to live in extreme places, where neither might easily live alone and where few other organisms can survive, such as bare rock faces, polar regions, tundra and desert.

The plant, the rock and the butterfly

Investigation of another plant, horseshoe vetch (*Hippocrepis comosa*) also reveals a close correlation with geology, in this case with belts of limestone rock. Take a look at its distribution map (below left), which shows that the plant's growth is confined to certain patches and bands within its climate zone reaching mainly across southern England. Such distinctive belt-like patterns hint at a subterranean connection with the rocks and strata that make up our landscape. A glance at a second map (below centre), which illustrates where chalk and limestone rocks come to the surface in the British Isles, and you'll see a clear correlation. The two maps are a near-perfect match in the south of England. The soils that cover these rocks are rich in lime and usually well-drained – the two things that horseshoe vetch really needs in order to grow well. Once again, the distribution of a plant mirrors the geology of the British Isles (see p.44).

If we now turn to a third map (below right), we can see a wider connection with the local wildlife, specifically with the chalkhill blue butterfly (*Polyommatus coridon*) whose caterpillars feed only on horseshoe vetch. The pattern of the butterfly's distribution

ABOVE Horseshoe vetch flourishes in southern England on lime-rich soil.

BELOW A sequence of maps revealing connections between the distribution patterns of horseshoe vetch (below left), limestone rocks (middle) and the chalkhill blue butterfly (right).

HORSESHOE VETCH
HIPPOCREPIS COMOSA
TODAY

LIMESTONE ROCK
TODAY

CHALKHILL
BLUE BUTTERFLY
POLYOMMATUS CORIDON
TODAY

nearly matches that of horseshoe vetch, revealing a direct
correlation in the occurrence of the two species – in fact,
the map for horseshoe vetch acts as a species indicator,
pin-pointing where we are most likely to find chalkhill
blue butterflies. Remarkably, the map for horseshoe vetch
provides three layers of information, showing not only what
we're likely to find below ground, but also the whereabouts
of other wild things in our landscape.

Modern interconnections

The lay of the land, the underlying nature of the landscape and
the interconnected community of wild things all provide vital clues
about plant distributions. Even closer to home, though, our own
interaction with the environment often plays a crucial role in shaping
the shifting patterns of distribution played out on the plant maps.
New discoveries are being reported all the time that don't just
inform us about the plants themselves, but provide clues about
our own twenty-first-century lifestyles, as the next case reveals.

TOP *Horseshoe vetch is
most common in chalk
and limestone grassland.
Here on Martin Down
in Wiltshire, it grows in
abundance with rare
plants, such as burnt
orchid* (Neotinea ustulata).

ABOVE *The largest of our
blue butterflies, the male
chalkhill blue is seen
flying mainly in August.
The flamboyant colour
of its wings attracts the
brown female butterfly.*

ABOVE *Mossy stonecrop (red) is not a moss at all, but a tiny flowering plant.*

BELOW *The maps reveal that this plant is spreading northwards, suggesting a link with climate change.*

The case of the rolling 'moss'

Tiny mossy stonecrop (*Crassula tillaea*) is on the move. For a long time, it was seen mainly on the light, acidic soils of East Anglia and the New Forest in southern England, both warm parts of the country with the right soil conditions for the plant to thrive. Now the maps for its distribution reveal that it's fanning out from these areas: in the last fifty years it has spread, popping up in southwest England, Wales and especially in northeastern Scotland.

Two things seem to be affecting its movements. Firstly, it's a species that enjoys the warmth. In fact, this little plant is really more at home in the Mediterranean, soaking up the sunshine, so here in the British Isles it's on the very edge of its northern range, only just tolerating our cool weather. As our climate has grown ever warmer during the last twenty years, however, mossy stonecrop appears to have become happier and to be spreading as a result.

Secondly, the exact location of the plant, as recorded by plant spotters, implies that we've played a part in its spread because it's turning up 'in the gravel of a car park', 'in the caravan park', 'all over the marina', 'in the lay-by beside a lake' and at the 'station car park'. Quite probably the seeds of this plant are getting around the

MOSSY STONECROP
CRASSULA TILLAEA

1962

TODAY

country on our car tyres. In Scotland, it's even made its way onto forestry tracks, spreading through the woods on the tyres of trucks and machinery.

Today, the map for mossy stonecrop hints at both climate change and our own influence in the plant's spread. It's a graphic example of how the fortunes of many plants are closely connected to our own actions and activities. Who knows, though, what mossy stonecrop's map will look like in another fifty years? The plant might have fanned out further, or it might have shrunk back to its former strongholds, depending on how the climate changes and whether we're still driving around as much. Only one thing is certain: the map *will* have changed. With global warming set to alter weather patterns dramatically and with an ever-growing population placing more and more demands on our land for food, housing and development, who can say what the next fifty years will bring?

It is these dynamic shifts and changes in the patterns of wild things that make plant detection so exciting. If everything were to stay the same, we'd have a dull old countryside. Some plants will go, others will come back and new ones will arrive. What's really important is that we keep looking, searching and finding wild things on the move.

A bird's eye view of the Wiltshire village of Lyneham in southern England vividly reveals some of the changes that have taken place in our countryside. The village (centre), along with its patchwork of intensively farmed fields, has grown over the last sixty years mainly to serve the Royal Air Force (RAF) base (centre left), which is itself expanding.

MAPPING THE MOSSES AND LICHENS

Given the minute size of lichens and mosses, the idea of recording every single one across the whole country might seem an impossible task that only the very keen (or crazy) person would attempt. However, when moss lovers and lichen fans got together through the Moss Exchange Club (now the British Bryological Society) in the late 1800s, and later through the British Lichen Society in 1958, this is precisely what they set out to do. Members trekked off across the country to record the location of everything mossy and lichen-like that they came across. Mountains were scaled, beaches were combed and woodlands were rifled.

All species found in the wild were recorded by name and location, as well as the recorder's name. Sometimes a small sample taken in the field would be dried in a paper packet and added to the herbarium. Today these specimens provide invaluable data, allowing us to track any changes in the size, shape and location of individual species.

Casting the net wider

These early surveys were carried out by a small band of dedicated enthusiasts and naturalists who often focused on their favourite habitats or local area rather than covering the whole country. Although their research revealed the importance of certain habitats for mosses and lichens, it left the country only patchily surveyed. To widen the net, government agencies stepped in and ensured that what were considered important sites would be surveyed – from the ancient sarsen stones of Pewsey Downs in Wiltshire, southern England, to Horner Wood in Somerset, southwest England.

Today our knowledge of the distribution of these species is better than ever. The British Lichen Society holds more than 1.5 million records of lichens, while the British Bryological Society has more than 2 million reports of bryophytes (mosses and liverworts). These documents have recently been checked for accuracy to ensure that the species name is correct and the location likely. If still seemingly solid and reliable, the record is entered into a database that is made publicly available and continuously updated.

A drystone wall in Cumbria covered in lichens, including the aptly named map lichen (below). Dried herbarium samples (bottom) contain a shrivelled piece of lichen that might have been gathered in the field hundreds of years ago. These remarkable packets hold the secrets of yesteryear, telling us what individual species looked like and where they were found.

The sarsen stones (top) in Wiltshire, southern England, provide rich pickings for lichen enthusiasts. Composed of rare rock types, dating from the last Ice Age, they support many unusual lichens. More recently, a lichen that has responded positively to nitrogen pollutants and undergone a corresponding boom is Xanthoria parietina *(right).*

Mapping critical change

The tiny size of lichens and mosses makes it unlikely that we will ever have a complete record of all species from every single point in time. Because of this, records are often analysed at the 10km-square scale, rather than at finer scales, as it gives us a coarser understanding of where wild things are growing and how distributions are changing.

As an example of the difference in perspective, the broader overview gained at the 10km-square scale might flag up the wholesale disappearance of a lichen from forests in general, whereas a closer scale, for example 1km, might highlight something of more local significance, such as the disappearance of a lichen from one tree as a result of natural processes while its fellows remain on trees in a woodland nearby. Taking the broader view helps us to pick up larger-scale trends of national concern – for example shifting distributions that might be part of a widespread change –

rather than local happenings. Monitoring in this way, we are quickly able to determine if a species is becoming rare or endangered.

Monitoring lichen movements

The environmental problems that we face today, such as habitat loss, pollution and climate change, all put pressures on the places where lichens and mosses like to live. As a result, these species are often one of the first to respond to environmental change and to signal that there might be trouble further down the food chain if we don't put things right. Because these species are so sensitive, it is vital that we continue to monitor and record where they are living.

True, it may be a never-ending task, but the changing nature of moss and lichen distributions means that it's now an ideal time to go exploring and see what you can find. You might turn up a new record for your garden, your county or even your country. It's an exciting time start looking!

INTO THE GREAT OUTDOORS

Over the next few chapters, we'll explore some of the habitats that have seen most change. From woodlands to roadsides, from mountain tops to fields of wheat and barley, the maps for each plant open a window onto the natural world, revealing what's going on, where and why.

We'll encounter many wild things – some iconic old friends, such as poppies and bluebells (see pp.57–71); others stranger than fiction and hidden from the naked eye, such as waterbears (see pp.114–15). We'll follow the trail of plants that are on the increase, such as prickly lettuce (*Lactuca serriola*), and investigate why others, such as burnt orchid (*Neotinea ustulata*), are on the way out (see pp.106, 215). You'll never look at your surroundings, with its multitude of wild things, in quite the same way again.

Chris and Lottie explore the rugged coast of Anglesey, North Wales, home to Danish scurvygrass (foreground), a plant on the move (see chapter 3).

LEFT AND BELOW The Wild Things *team, Trevor, Chris, Sally and Lotty scour the country looking for evidence of change in our wild plants.*

CHAPTER TWO
WOODLANDS

PREVIOUS PAGE With their dappled light and cool, humid air, temperate woodlands provide the right conditions for a wide range of plants, from tiny mosses to exotic orchids.

BELOW At Cwm Mynach in Snowdonia, North Wales, native bluebells flourish between gnarled old oaks. Such ancient woodlands are especially rich in wild things.

There are 3.1 million hectares of woodland in the British Isles, representing nearly 13 per cent of the total land area. That's a lot of forest, equivalent to about 7.6 million football pitches.

But only 1.3 per cent of our woodland is wildlife-rich ancient forest, and around one in five (18 per cent) of our forest flowers are now under threat. Even quite common forest plants, such as wood anemone (*Anemone nemorosa*), are disappearing. Within our lifetime, one of our favourite, most familiar habitats is changing.

It's not the trees, though … at least not the native ones. Apart from elms that have succumbed to Dutch elm disease since the 1960s, a disaster that might now be repeated for ash trees, the distribution maps for oak, beech, alder and birch, for instance, have shown little change over the last fifty years. Some of our non-native trees such as conifers have, however, increased significantly. So what exactly is going on?

Our woods are more than just their trees. While the trees might form the 'skeleton' of a forest, its 'flesh and muscle' are provided by an astonishing variety of other wild things …

NATIVE BLUEBELL
HYACINTHOIDES NON-SCRIPTA

TODAY

BLUEBELLS

Our native bluebell (*Hyacinthoides non-scripta*) is our most iconic woodland plant – in fact British forests are home to up to 70 per cent of the world's 'British' bluebell population. Although native bluebells do grow elsewhere, such as in France and northern Spain, it's only in the British Isles that they flourish in such wonderfully dense bluebell dells. But for how long will this last? Our most treasured bluebell dells could now be under threat from a foreign invader.

A healthy mass of coloured dots, representing our native bluebell, spreads across the distribution map for this plant today.

A Spanish invasion

Something has been happening over the past fifty years that has caused quite a stir among botanists. Although the most recent distribution map for our native bluebell shows that it is found throughout the British Isles (see p.57), if we look at another map (below), we can see that, all over the country, a new kid is appearing on the block. Outbreaks of blue are emerging in unexpected places, outside the ancient woods and dells that we all associate so closely with our native bluebells.

The newcomer – popularly known as the Spanish bluebell (*Hyacinthoides hispanica*) after its main country of origin – is threatening to change the character of our woodlands forever and it's on the march. The trouble is that, once this new variety gets in among our native bluebells, there's not much we can do to stop it taking over. So why are these newcomers spreading, and where? What exactly do we stand to lose if their march continues?

Spanish bluebells were first brought over from continental Europe in the late seventeenth century to feed an increasing desire

The sparsely dotted map for the Spanish bluebell in 1962 (below left) shows how uncommon it was in the wild fifty years ago. It has since spread rapidly and now appears on roadsides, hedge banks and woodland edges throughout lowland Britain (below right).

SPANISH BLUEBELL
HYACINTHOIDES HISPANICA

1962

TODAY

by British gardeners to grow as many different plants as possible, especially any new, foreign varieties that would make their gardens look special. The Spanish bluebells were greatly admired, with their clusters of big, chunky, pale blue flowers that faced outwards from tall, upright stems. The new bluebells were vigorous, too, with their fat, broad leaves forming clumps that doubled in size in just a few years; and they had a wonderful way of springing up all over the garden as their seeds took hold, generating many new plants that were entirely free. Our own native bluebell, by contrast, had a reputation for being difficult to 'get going', usually fading away after a while and taking years to flower from seed. No wonder that gardeners of the time preferred the Spanish bluebell to our own.

The popular new bluebells flourished in gardens for over 220 years before they finally made their escape into the wild at the turn of the twentieth century when, in 1909, they were first reported growing in the wild in the British Isles. In other words, Spanish bluebells had jumped over the garden wall and cut loose, getting into places where we'd never intended them to be (see pp.63–4).

BELOW LEFT Naturalized Spanish bluebells, which have escaped into the wild in the British Isles, form vigorous clumps and tend to spread easily.

BELOW At home in Spain, Spanish bluebells are sometimes more delicate than their naturalized counterparts in the British Isles.

A stem of a hybrid bluebell, with its distinctive mid-blue colour and bell-shaped flowers.

The making of a new bluebell

Even more worryingly, by the time that the Spanish bluebell had jumped the wall, another new bluebell had appeared. It was a cross between our native and the Spanish bluebell, since the two quickly cross-bred once gardeners had introduced the newcomers into our gardens. The result of their union was an entirely new plant, the hybrid bluebell (*Hyacinthoides x massartiana*) (see diagram below).

Cross-breeding and back-crossing

Plants really do have a tendency to be a little bit promiscuous and, unlike animals, many will readily cross-breed with closely related species, given half the chance. The hybrid outcome usually combines traits from both parents. Occasionally, the new offspring will inherit the best bits (or genes) from each parent, resulting in extra-strong plants that are said to have 'hybrid vigour'.

Hybrids are also often able to cross again with either of their parents (with, for instance, either the pure Spanish or the pure native variety), a process known as 'back-crossing'. Over time, this continual and repeated crossing between all the offspring creates a complete range of intermediates, or what's called a 'hybrid swarm'.

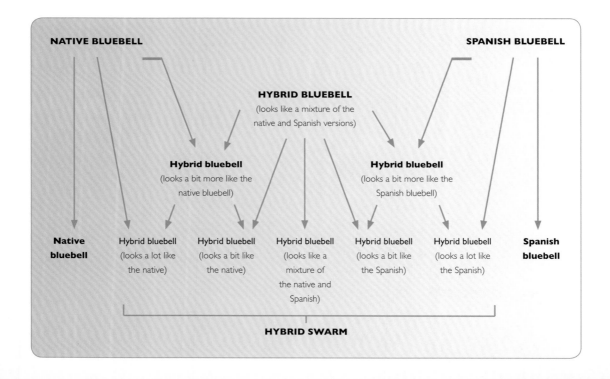

HYBRID BLUEBELL
HYACINTHOIDES X MASSARTIANA

1962

TODAY

People soon found that the new hybrids grew well in gardens and they started to become very widely available, often being mis-sold as 'English bluebells' to make them sound more appealing. Adding to their attraction, hybrid bluebells were also available in colours other than blue, including both pink and white, which became particularly popular. Our native British bluebell also produces very beautiful pure white flowers in the wild, but pink flowers are extremely rare; pink bluebells are almost always hybrids.

Not only did the hybrids flourish in gardens but, before long, large numbers had followed the Spanish variety over the wall into the wild. Initially, it wasn't realized that it was actually the hybrids that were escaping, as most escapes at the time were assumed to be Spanish. It was not until 1963 that hybrids were first spotted in the wild and not until 1987 that botanists registered the full scale of their spread. Hybrids are now moving across the country so fast that the latest map (above right) is only just keeping up with them. The result over the years has been a perfect storm for our native bluebell.

ABOVE Although first discovered in the wild in the early 1960s, the hybrid bluebell was largely overlooked until 1987. We were caught napping as it spread rapidly across the countryside, threatening our native bluebells.

OPPOSITE BOTTOM Constant cross-breeding and back-crossing between native, Spanish and hybrid bluebells eventually generates a range of intermediate strains known as a 'hybrid swarm'.

FLOWERING TIMES

	J	F	M	A	M	J	J	A	S	O	N	D
Native bluebell	✿	✿	✿	✿	✿	✿	✿	✿	✿	✿	✿	✿
Spanish bluebell	✿	✿	✿	✿	✿	✿	✿	✿	✿	✿	✿	✿
Hybrid bluebell	✿	✿	✿	✿	✿	✿	✿	✿	✿	✿	✿	✿

Spot the non-natives

Identifying which bluebells grow in which areas can be tricky, especially with hybrids. The table below helps to tell the different bluebells apart. Look out for hybrid swarms!

CHARACTER	NATIVE BLUEBELL	HYBRID BLUEBELL	SPANISH BLUEBELL
Scent	Strong, sweet, carries on the air	Slight, not carrying far	None or mild and unpleasant
Pollen colour	White or cream	Pale blue to blue	Blue
Flower colour	Very dark blue, rarely white	Dark to pale blue, often white or pink	Pale blue
Flower shape	Narrow, tubular with petals flaring at the base	Narrow to bell-shaped	An open bell shape
Flower spike	Nodding over at the tip	Nodding to upright	Upright
Flower arrangement	Almost all hang on one side of the stem	Some hang on one side but the lower flowers hang all round the stem	All hang all round the stem
Leaves	Very narrow, 1–1.5cm wide	Broad, 1.5–3cm wide	Very broad, often more than 3cm wide

The new bluebells are on the move

Hybrid and Spanish bluebells are now spreading further afield, colonizing surprising places where they've not been seen before. Today, the non-natives are widely found on urban roadsides, waste tips and woodland edges, in churchyards and on cliffs and beaches by the coast – in fact, on any bits of unused land and wherever people and gardens are found.

Our native bluebell, by contrast, is a woodland plant. Or, rather, it's a plant of humidity, preferring a damp spot with warm, moist air. In much of the drier south and east of England, native bluebells are almost exclusively woodland plants, confined to the protection of shade provided by a canopy of leaves. Head north and west, though, and you'll see that, as the climate gets wetter and cloudier, bluebells move out of the woods and start appearing in the open. In certain areas, they even grow on exposed hillsides, heaths and sea cliffs, where stands of bracken (*Pteridium aquilinum*) often provide welcome cover: their fronds shade the bluebells, like the canopy of a dwarf woodland.

ABOVE LEFT Starting from bulbs that were initially planted, hybrid bluebells often spread to form dense stands in churchyards.

ABOVE Emerging fronds of bracken mimic a woodland canopy, providing shade for the native bluebells beneath.

Why are the new bluebells spreading further afield?

They've got the best bits from both parents.

Remember the genes that were shared between the Spanish and native bluebells – the 'best bits' gained from each parent that produced 'hybrid vigour' (see p.60)? This vigour makes the new hybrid bluebells much stronger and more competitive than the native plant. They can stand up to tougher neighbours, which means that they're more likely to grow among coarse grasses on roadsides and along woodland edges.

The newcomers: hybrid bluebells (below) and Spanish bluebells (bottom).

They keep getting out.

The vigour and ability of the newcomers to spread in our gardens means that they can quickly take over beds and borders, becoming quite a pest. So they're often dug up and thrown out with other garden rubbish, usually over the road onto the opposite verge, on the edge of woodlands, or into hedgerows. Casual fly-tipping of garden waste is the major mechanism for their escape, which is why we find so many new bluebells now growing along our road networks throughout the British Isles. Once out, the newcomers continue their march.

What if their march continues?

The distribution maps show that Spanish and hybrid bluebells have spread rapidly in urban and suburban areas where there is a higher density of population and, therefore, a greater risk of people tossing plants over the garden wall. In many cities, it can now be hard to find native bluebells, but non-natives abound.

From the distribution maps (see pp.58, 61), the increase in Spanish and hybrid bluebells looks set to continue and they are increasingly being encountered in more rural and remote places in the countryside, too. The main worry is that, once the non-natives reach our ancient woodlands, there will be a real risk of our losing one of the most iconic sights in our landscape – the British bluebell dell.

The sweet smell of bluebell dells

What we stand to lose in all of this is not simply the enchanting sight of bluebell dells, but also their stunning aroma. The newcomers lack that same distinctive fragrance and, in fact, they hardly smell at all. Wondering why our natives smell so sweetly, the *Wild Things* team undertook an experiment that would, for the first time ever, pinpoint the exact characteristics of our native bluebell's special scent. It produced some amazing results that might hold the clue as to why this flower's unique fragrance means so much to us (see pp.68–9).

A quintessential bluebell dell, carpeted with deep-blue native bluebells, which produce a strong, sweet scent that carries on the air.

THE NATION'S FAVOURITE

The latest research shows that the British Isles are home to up to 70 per cent of the world's 'British' bluebells (right). Although our native bluebells also grow in parts of Europe, it's only in Britain and Ireland that they flourish in the incredibly dense bluebell dells that are found in ancient forests (see pp.72–5).

Our native bluebell is, quite possibly, our most iconic flower. In a poll organized by the plant conservation charity Plantlife to name an emblematic wild flower for each British county, everyone chose the native bluebell. In the end, it had to be removed from the competition, as its popularity outstripped all other flowers. The humble British bluebell was instead placed on top of the podium in first place, taking the title of the nation's favourite flower.

WHY DO FLOWERS SMELL?

Plants produce flowers for one reason only – to attract pollinators, such as bees, butterflies and other insects, which go from flower to flower in search of a nutritious meal of nectar and pollen (right). As they feast, their bodies get dusted with the plant's powdery pollen – fine grains containing sperm cells produced by the male part of the flower. When the insect alights on another plant, some of the pollen on its body brushes off and finds its way to the female part of a new flower, enabling fertilization to take place. The result is seed and the next generation of plants.

Scent acts as a long-range signal carried on the wind and, once on the final approach to a flower, an insect is guided in by a barrage of visual clues, such as colour and shape. Flowers have evolved a vast range of scents to attract insects. Once an insect learns that a particular smell is associated with a reward, it just keeps coming back for more. Floral scents sometimes mimic an insect's pheromones (the chemicals used to attract a mate for reproduction), in which case an insect might think it's in for more than just a meal. Sometimes a scent mimics other things, which aren't always pleasant. Owl-midges, for example, are attracted to the strange flowers of lords-and-ladies (*Arum maculatum*) by a faecal smell, suggesting the ideal place to lay their eggs.

The case of the thieving bumblebee

Like other flowers, our native bluebell produces its special scent, along with its striking colour, to attract pollinators (see above). Scent and colour combine to broadcast an irresistible message: 'Over here, guys, for a sugar-and-pollen hit to keep you going.' And so the pollinators come. Flowering early in the year, bluebells are an especially valuable source of food to bumblebees and other insects. The early feast of nutritious nectar and pollen is like a big, fat breakfast for many insects emerging from their long winter hibernation. Bumblebees are especially partial to a bit of bluebell but they've had a bad press, as they're often accused of being nectar thieves. They are said to 'steal' nectar by biting a hole in the top of a flower. In this way, they don't get dusted in pollen or go on to pollinate other flowers, which is how insects usually 'repay' a flower for its nectar. But no bees have been caught thieving nectar from British bluebells, only from the panicled bluebell (*Mertensia paniculata*) in North America. It's a case of mistaken identity – our bumblebee stands wrongly accused!

Picking wild bluebells: the do's and don'ts

It might be tempting to pick a handful of wild bluebells in the woods (right), but are you sure that you're allowed to? There's much confusion over the law on our native bluebells, so here's the low-down on what you can and can't do.

Can you pick wild native bluebells?

As long as you are not taking up the bulb as well, it's not usually an offence to pick native bluebell flowers if they are:

● growing in the wild;
● for your own use and not intended for sale;
● not on protected land, such as nature reserves;
● not on protected council-owned land, including parks, roundabouts or verges.

All wild plants are the property of someone, so it's always best to get the landowner's permission beforehand. This is true of all wild flowers, except for a special group of very vulnerable plants that cannot be picked without a licence (see p.187).

Can you dig up wild native bluebells?

Uprooting bluebells is quite distinct from simply picking the flowers. Under the Wildlife and Countryside Act (1981), it is illegal to uproot any wild plant in Britain without permission from the landowner or occupier. If you pick a bluebell flower, and the bulb and roots come up with it, you might have committed an offence!

For native bluebells, the law is extra tough on digging up bulbs. This is because there have been cases where entire woodlands and hillsides have been stripped of their bulbs in order to sell them. In 2007 two men were fined £7,000 for selling 200,000 native bluebell bulbs collected from a site on the Llŷn Peninsular in North Wales. Since the maximum penalty is £5,000 per bulb, the fine could have been as much as a billion pounds.

Can you collect seed?

You can collect small amounts of seed from plants in the wild to grow in your own garden, but you cannot collect any amount for commercial use without a special licence.

Trevor gathers wild bluebells with Lottie at Lickey Hills Country Park, Birmingham – with the landowner's permission but without uprooting the bulbs. Plunging the cut flower stems into a bucket of iced water for an hour or so will help them to last much longer indoors, where their scent will fill a room.

What's in the whiff?

Our native British bluebell has an incredibly complex smell, which is as baffling as it is beguiling. The plant has invested heavily in a powerful scent to help attract its pollinators, but it's not just the bees that love the scent. A flowering woodland dell is an iconic springtime sight, memorable for the sheer spectacle of all those flowers, as well as the powerful experience of their scent.

This experiment was designed to reveal what could be lost if the odourless Spanish bluebell were to take over our woodland dells (see pp.58–65). For the first time ever, the *Wild Things* team were able to analyse the exact characteristics of this special scent that is unique to British woodlands.

The equipment
1 x whiff of native bluebell
1 x whiff of Spanish bluebell
1 x funnel
1 x nose (and some expert equipment!)

The method
To capture the unique bluebell scent, a technique called solid-phase microextraction (SPME) was used. First, delicate glass funnels were placed around each flower; then a small syringe was inserted into the flower head to collect the scent sample. Next, the samples were sent off to Bangor University in North Wales for analysis.

On the scent of a bluebell, Trevor collects the smell samples from native bluebells in an ancient woodland.

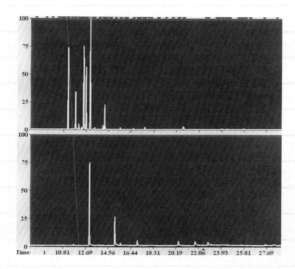

Comparative graphs reveal contrasting scent peaks for native bluebells (top) and Spanish bluebells (bottom).

The scent revealed

In the comparative graphs (above), the top shows results for our native bluebell, while the bottom illustrates those for the Spanish species. Looking at the top graph first, it's clear from the number of peaks that the native's scent is packed full of different ingredients, known as volatile organic compounds. Each peak stands for a different volatile organic compound that contributes another scent note to the flower. The main cluster of high peaks in the top graph represents a family of chemical compounds, known as monoterpenes. What's most revealing is that the same high monoterpene peaks occur with fruits, such as lemon, apple, mango and lychees, as well as with ginger and freshly mown grass.

On the lower graph, by contrast, far fewer high peaks appear, suggesting a narrower range of volatile organic compounds. With just a few monoterpenes present, the Spanish scent is less rich and complex than that of our native plant.

THE SCIENCE

What the experiment confirmed is the very intricate complexity of our native bluebell's scent. It can't be pinned down to one particular fragrance or formula. It's a chemical soup and a highly complex and intriguing one at that. The scents to which it corresponds most closely all emanate from things that refresh and revitalize us. So, when you walk into a woodland dell, it's this heady mix of invigorating scents that you'll first start to detect. It wafts on the air, drawing the pollinating bees into the wood, into shady spots that they'd usually avoid.

But this spectacle of the British spring is now under threat from an imposter that barely uses scent at all, as is clear from the graph for the Spanish bluebell (left), with hardly any peaks. It just flashes its colourful floral skirt to charm the bees in, but offers no correspondingly appealing scent; and yet this fairly scentless flower is now spreading itself around, possibly even moving into our richly scented woodland dells.

The results of the experiment at least help us to understand the appealing fragrance of our native buebell. Its seemingly 'fruity' notes help to explain why the experience of being in a woodland, with its powerful bluebell fragrance, seems so refreshing and uplifting. The scent's complex cocktail of compounds is incredibly difficult, if not impossible, to replicate accurately. So when the scent of a bluebell dell is experienced in the woods, it really is unlike anything else.

The fresh zingy scents of lemons, lychees, apples, lemongrass and mangoes share some of the same chemical ingredients as those of our native bluebell.

Bluebell watch

When the spread of the hybrid bluebell first became apparent in 1987, there was a bit of a panic over the future of our native bluebell, with fears that it would soon be lost forever and the character of our bluebell dells changed for all time as the genes from the hybrid made their way into pure populations. The current evidence, however, indicates that, once hybrids arrive at the edge of a wood, their exchange of pollen with native bluebells within the woods is very slow. There are still huge areas of woodland full of native bluebells, where the populations remain pure – for the time being at least.

Perhaps, though, the non-natives are just massing on the front line before spreading and increasing slowly. Is there a critical point that has to be reached before the non-native genes can more easily get into our native gene pool? If we've already lost most of our urban bluebells, a similar fate could befall those in our countryside. We don't yet know but, if we do want to save our native bluebells, what's really important is that we remain vigilant – especially in and around those bluebell dells that we love so much. In the meantime, we should do all we can to stop the spread of the non-natives.

STOP THE SPREAD OF NON-NATIVE BLUEBELLS

Help curb the spread of non-native bluebells by taking a few simple precautions:

- Grow only native bluebells bought from reputable sources.

- Dispose of non-native bluebells carefully.

- Don't throw non-native bluebells into the wild.

- Compost non-native bluebells with care, allowing the bulbs to dry out thoroughly before composting.

Trevor on the front line, with invading Spanish bluebells in the foreground, natives behind and some hybrids in between.

Light through the trees?

There is a final twist to the bluebell's tale. Spanish bluebells originated in southern Spain and Portugal, countries with warm, dry Mediterranean summers – in fact, just the climate that has been predicted for Britain if global warming continues. We might well wonder how Britain's three bluebells will fare in a warmer future? Spanish bluebells do seem better adapted to the hot, dry weather of their southern homelands, whereas our native bluebells might cope less well. Now that Pandora's Box has been opened, however, and the Spanish and hybrid versions have already taken such a hold in and around our cities, we should perhaps welcome the fact that they might survive the predicted climate change. If our own bluebells, by contrast, do suffer in the potentially hotter cities of the future, it would perhaps be better to have some kind of bluebell in our urban spaces than none at all. For the time being, though, we mustn't forget that we are the guardians of up to 70 per cent of the world's population of 'British' bluebells, both in our countryside and in our most treasured bluebell dells, so we really must keep a lookout.

A flush of native bluebells out on a windswept hilltop, thriving in the cool, wet climate of western Scotland.

ANCIENT WOODLANDS

Dense woodland once covered much of the British Isles, developing after the end of the last Ice Age around 10,000 years ago. Then, as early Britons settled during succeeding centuries, stretches of woodland were gradually felled for farming and dwelling until, by the time the Romans arrived in 54 BC, about half the original woodland had been cleared. Pockets of ancient wooded landscape still survive today in our oldest forests, such as Ty Canol Wood in Wales or Morrone Birkwood in Scotland (see pp.74–5). Ancient woodlands are places where time has almost stood still and, once lost, can never be recreated. Such forests are special; we can trace their roots back for generations.

For a forest to be officially classified as 'ancient woodland' in England, Wales and Northern Ireland, it should have been present since at least 1600 (in Scotland, since 1750). After 1600, it became common practice to plant new trees for timber, but any forests already present in 1600 (before new trees were planted) could have been maturing since at least the early Middle Ages, c.500–1100, and sometimes since the end of the last Ice Age, c.8000 BC.

An ancient woodland that has evolved through several hundred years offers an exceptionally rich variety of flowering plants, ferns, mosses, liverworts, fungi and lichens, which in turn provide habitat, shelter and food for a huge diversity of other wild things.

Ancient woodlands develop rich communities of plants, mosses, lichens and fungi over many hundreds of years.

Home to rare lichens and mosses

We can often identify ancient woodlands by looking closely at the lichens growing on forest trees. Certain communities, such as the lungwort or *Lobarion* lichens, are only found in woodlands that have remained undisturbed for a long time. These lichens are very particular about where they live and will only be found where the conditions for them are just right. Some of these species include witches' whiskers lichen (*Usnea florida*), lung lichen (*Lobaria pulmonaria*), western featherwort (*Plagiochila atlantica*) and plum-fruited felt lichen (*Degelia plumbea*). If you see them, you'll know that the woodland where they're growing has been at that very same spot continuously for many hundreds of years (see opposite). A certain suite of lichens can even indicate that the woodland has been present since at least Roman times, c.AD 300.

HOW TO SPOT AN ANCIENT WOODLAND

The presence of certain plants in a forest can help us to spot ancient woodlands. If you see any of these plants or lichens growing in your local forest, it's likely to be an ancient woodland, dating back to at least 1600 and possibly several hundred years earlier.

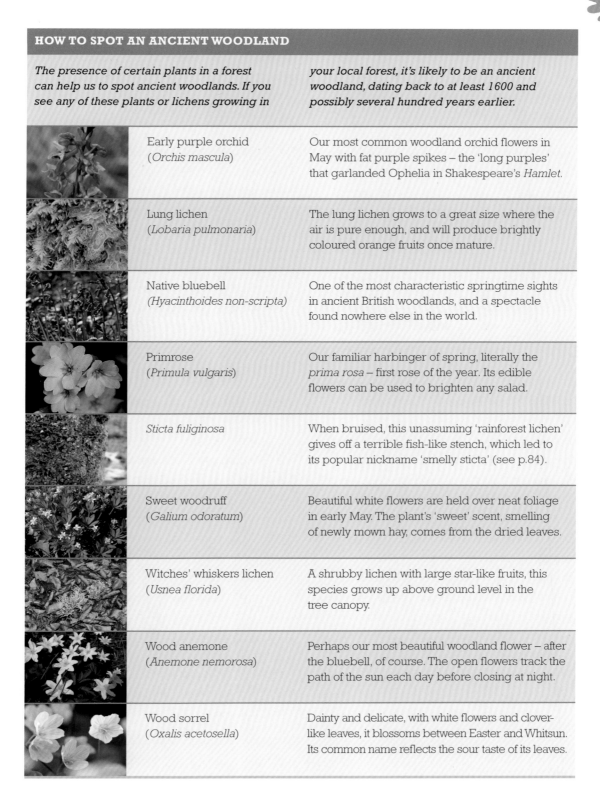

	Early purple orchid (*Orchis mascula*)	Our most common woodland orchid flowers in May with fat purple spikes – the 'long purples' that garlanded Ophelia in Shakespeare's *Hamlet*.
	Lung lichen (*Lobaria pulmonaria*)	The lung lichen grows to a great size where the air is pure enough, and will produce brightly coloured orange fruits once mature.
	Native bluebell (*Hyacinthoides non-scripta*)	One of the most characteristic springtime sights in ancient British woodlands, and a spectacle found nowhere else in the world.
	Primrose (*Primula vulgaris*)	Our familiar harbinger of spring, literally the *prima rosa* – first rose of the year. Its edible flowers can be used to brighten any salad.
	Sticta fuliginosa	When bruised, this unassuming 'rainforest lichen' gives off a terrible fish-like stench, which led to its popular nickname 'smelly sticta' (see p.84).
	Sweet woodruff (*Galium odoratum*)	Beautiful white flowers are held over neat foliage in early May. The plant's 'sweet' scent, smelling of newly mown hay, comes from the dried leaves.
	Witches' whiskers lichen (*Usnea florida*)	A shrubby lichen with large star-like fruits, this species grows up above ground level in the tree canopy.
	Wood anemone (*Anemone nemorosa*)	Perhaps our most beautiful woodland flower – after the bluebell, of course. The open flowers track the path of the sun each day before closing at night.
	Wood sorrel (*Oxalis acetosella*)	Dainty and delicate, with white flowers and clover-like leaves, it blossoms between Easter and Whitsun. Its common name reflects the sour taste of its leaves.

FIVE ANCIENT WOODLANDS

1 Sherwood Forest, England

Centuries before the medieval hero Robin Hood first sheltered beneath Sherwood's leafy boughs, the forest was home to some of England's most ancient trees – in fact, more than 900 of Sherwood's trees are at least 600 years old. Many veteran oaks, such as the pedunculate (*Quercus robur*) and sessile (*Q. petraea*), survive today, including the major oak, which could be 1,000 years old. The forest itself dates to the end of the last Ice Age. Its extensive woods, although now much reduced since the time of Robin Hood, still cover an area equivalent to more than 1,000 football pitches.

2 The New Forest, England

At nearly 12,000 years old, the New Forest in Hampshire is really not so new. Actually, the 'new' bit in its name refers to its establishment as a royal hunting forest in *c*.1079. As the largest remaining tract of forest and heath in southern England, *c*.190km wide, it is home to a fantastic array of rare wild things, such as mole crickets, the New Forest cicada and wild gladiolus (*Gladiolus illyricus*). Spotting such rarities brings a certain thrill to a day in the forest.

3 Wistman's Wood, England

The stuff of ghost stories, Wistman's Wood on Dartmoor is Devon's oldest forest. Dating back to *c*.8000 BC, it once stretched across the West Dart Valley. Now a boulder-strewn hillside relict, it is covered in gnarled and stunted ancient oaks, most no more than 3m tall, dripping with mosses and lichens. The wood's name apparently stems from *wisht,* meaning eerie or haunted, and local folklore has it that the Wisht Hounds chase sinners across the moors. Be careful if you visit!

4 Ty Canol Wood, Wales

From its oak-dominated canopy to its moss-strewn boulders, Ty Canol Wood epitomizes how our ancient woodlands have always developed in partnership with farmers and foresters. A tradition of livestock grazing kept the canopy open, allowing light to flood the forest floor, which in turn enabled more than 400 different species of lichens and mosses to flourish, such as witches' whiskers lichen, which grows on sessile oak. The wood is equally rich in other plants, such as Wilson's filmy fern (*Hymenophyllum wilsonii*). Today, sheep, cattle and ponies maintain the ancient link between the forest and local farms.

5 Morrone Birkwood, Scotland

As 'birk' is Scots for 'birch', it's not surprising that Morrone Birkwood is one of the finest birchwoods in the British Isles. It is also home to some of the largest and most diverse stands of juniper in the country, as well as many plants that have remained unchanged since the last Ice Age, such as twinflower (*Linnaea borealis*) and globeflower (*Trollius europaeus*). Morrone's outstanding flora, for which you'd have to travel to Norway to find anything remotely similar, is a result of the wood's unusual lime-rich and fertile soil.

The British Isles offer a variety of ancient woodland haunts, not only legendary forests, such as Wistman's Wood (3), but also lesser-known relics, such as Ty Canol (4).

THE GHOST ORCHID

The ghost orchid (*Epipogium aphyllum*) is a plant of deep woodland, typically growing in the dense shade of beech trees. It really is quite strange, as it produces no green leaves and is not usually visible above ground. Then, seemingly from nowhere, a stem erupts from the soil, carrying very curious flowers: slightly flesh-coloured above, with greenish, dangly bits below. It's all rather macabre and other-worldly, as implied by the plant's name. In Britain, this curious-looking orchid has only ever been found in ten sites. However, its ghostly appearances have always been erratic and many years can pass without any sight of its flowers.

By the new millennium, the ghost orchid seemed to be petering out. There had been just three 'recent' sightings of the plant: in 1979, it had been found in the wild in Oxfordshire; in 1982, in the Welsh Borders; and in 1987, in Buckinghamshire. Although there were rumours of later sightings, which cannot be ruled out given the plant's will-o'-the-wisp history, they were never substantiated. Botanists braced themselves for the worst – extinction. The last remaining dots on the distribution map would have to be removed.

HOW CAN A PLANT LIVE ENTIRELY UNDERGROUND?

Like so many other woodland plants, the ghost orchid (right) develops a very special relationship with a fungus. Instead of growing normal leaves and roots, it sprouts a branching stem underground, which looks a bit like a coral. The orchid allows the fungus to infect this coral-like structure, with the fungal mycelium (a network of fine white filaments) penetrating the cells of the underground stem. In this way, the orchid gets 'tapped into' the fungus' huge underground mycelium, which in turn is tapped into the roots of nearby trees, and basically lives off the food and nutrients provided by the trees and fungus.

GHOST ORCHID
EPIPOGIUM APHYLLUM

1962

The Ghost Hunters

Then, in the same way that the orchid grows beneath the surface, an underground network of 'Ghost Hunters' sprang up in the early 1980s. Soon secret Internet forums were established and coded messages exchanged. There were rumours and counter-rumours of the ghost's spectral reappearance. Finding the orchid remained the holiest of Holy Grails for British orchidophiles (people dedicated to orchids), and expert botanists determined to keep on looking.

Sadly, after years of no sightings, the ghost was finally declared extinct in 2005. But, as with all good ghost stories, there was more to come. Eventually, the orchid sleuths cracked the secret of this

The sparse dots on the plant map for the rare ghost orchid show where it once grew. Of all our wild plants, none has attracted such secrecy, rumour and detective work. The true story of its unexpected rediscovery in 2010, after twenty-three years' absence, is stranger than fiction.

Five years after being declared extinct, the ghost orchid mysteriously reappeared in the autumn of 2010, before falling victim to a hungry slug. The exact site of its miraculous return remains a closely guarded secret.

enigmatic plant. With careful detective work, they examined weather conditions in countries where the orchid still regularly appears, such as the Black Forest in Germany. They noticed that it flowered best following very cold, dry winters. The plant is what's called a 'continental species', one that feels most at home in the climate of Central Europe. In other words, it prefers to endure deep cold under a blanket of snow before emerging for the warmth of a continental summer.

Enter the Big Freeze, the punishing winter of 2009–10 when the British Isles experienced a semi-continental climate, with months of sub-zero temperatures. It was the coldest winter since 1987 – the last time that the ghost orchid had appeared. Could this climate possibly be what the plant needed? The orchid detectives staked out ten possible sites and visited each regularly throughout the following summer. Nothing surfaced.

Then, in late September of 2010, a warm period arrived. In bare mud on a sloping forest floor and in the deep shade of hazels and oaks, what looked like a snowflake appeared on the ground, barely visible. Was it a single flower, or just an apparition? On closer inspection, it proved to be real, and the orchid that had remained unseen for twenty-three years and been declared extinct, reappeared from the dead. It was never extinct, just lying dormant.

The plant was quickly photographed and verified but, alas, a few days later, its stem was eaten in the night by a slug and the orchid collapsed. It has not been seen since – a very ghostly encounter!

WOODLAND ORCHIDS

Most people think of orchids as tropical plants that need steaming jungles and endless rain, but we have many varied species in Britain: fifty-two, in fact, including the ghost orchid. British orchids belong to the same family as their flamboyant tropical cousins but, unlike them, don't grow up in the trees. Seventeen of the British species are woodland orchids, thriving in the shade or dappled semi-shade of forests. Most are quite rare, such as the lady orchid (*Orchis purpurea*), but the more common broad-leaved helleborine (*Epipactis helleborine*), twayblade (*Listera ovata*) and common spotted orchid (*Dactylorhiza fuchsii*), shown here, are worth keeping an eye out for.

HART'S-TONGUE FERN

Modern developments in agriculture, road networks, urban growth and conifer-planting have all impacted on our ancient broadleaved woodlands, which have decreased over the last fifty years. The distribution maps show that, in general, not many native woodland plants are on the increase. Just a few, though, such as hart's-tongue fern (*Asplenium scolopendrium*), are flourishing. The fern has spread northwards in the last fifty years, especially in northeast England and Scotland. What could be the cause of its expansion?

Like most ferns, hart's-tongue needs damp conditions in which to thrive and reproduce. In moist, shady spots on the forest floor, the fern's reproductive spores grow into tiny, flat, leaf-like structures (gametophytes), which produce female egg cells and male sperm cells. To fertilize the egg cell, the sperm cell swims across the surface of the gametophyte in a thin film of water. Successful fertilization results in the growth of a fern-like plant (a sporophyte), which matures and within a few years generates new spores.

Unlike most ferns, the fronds of hart's-tongue (inset) are broad and strap-like, resembling the tongue of an adult male deer, as implied by the fern's common name. Unlike many woodland plants, hart's-tongue fern has spread dramatically in the last fifty years, as its paired maps reveal.

HART'S-TONGUE FERN
ASPLENIUM SCOLOPENDRIUM

1962

TODAY

OPPOSITE: The decline of green hound's-tongue over the last fifty years is apparent from the distribution pattern shown on these paired maps for the plant. It is now thought to be extinct in nine English counties.

ABOVE A member of the borage family, green hound's-tongue grows on alkaline soil in open woodland.

Since hart's-tongue fern needs such moist, shady conditions in which to reproduce and thrive, its ideal home might well be on the increase as many of our forests are now left to grow wild: for the more we leave our native woodlands unmanaged, the more their canopies will close over, blocking out the sun, which in turn will lead to wetter conditions on the ground where these ferns thrive.

While the increase in damp, shady woodland partly explains the fern's spread, its march northwards suggests something else, possibly that it is responding to climate change. In the British Isles, our winters are becoming wetter and milder, while the 'growing season' has lengthened with spring coming earlier and autumn later each year. In this new climate, hart's-tongue fern has moved into more open woodland and even out onto walls. As it never liked the late spring frosts of previous years that could damage its freshly unfurled fronds, hart's-tongue seems to be one plant that's loving our milder, wetter climate.

GREEN HOUND'S-TONGUE

Green hound's-tongue (*Cynoglossum germanicum*) is one of our rarest woodland plants. It has declined dramatically during the last 100 years and is now lost from large parts of southern England where it once grew in ash and oak woods. The plant today lives on in only eight localities in Surrey, Gloucestershire and Oxfordshire in England. Due to the scale of its decline, it is now regarded as Critically Endangered. The largest populations survive in Surrey, but even these have been dwindling as the woodlands have matured and the canopy has closed over in the past fifty years.

Just as people feared the worst, though, the plant revived unexpectedly after the infamous Great Storm of October 1987, when hurricane-force winds of 190km per hour slammed into southern England, bringing down an estimated 15 million trees, including large areas of mature woodland. Green hound's-tongue loved it, though. After the storm, light flooded through to the forest floor around the felled trees, and huge populations of green hound's-tongue appeared, with many thousands of plants flowering and setting their seeds. Since then, the number at some sites has declined as the forests have closed over once more, but the seeds are still there in the soil, waiting patiently for the next Great Storm.

GREEN HOUND'S-TONGUE
CYNOGLOSSUM GERMANICUM

1962

TODAY

WHEN GIANTS FALL

We tend to imagine that most woodland plants like to grow in the dark of a shaded forest. Actually, like all plants, most need quite a bit of light. Left to their own devices, though, forests can become dark and dense as trees of all ages reach their full height. The forest's greatest trees, or 'sentinels', can grow immensely tall, sometimes more than 60m. As the trees reach for the skies, the forest canopy closes over, blocking out the light; and as the light goes, so do the plants.

When the oldest of the giant sentinels die, however, they crash to the ground, opening up huge gaps in the canopy. Light floods to the forest floor and the seeds of dormant flowers suddenly wake and grow, reaching for the light while it lasts, before the canopy closes over again.

WILD WORLDS

A psychedelic blaze in the woods

Under the cover of darkness, we can reveal something strange taking place in the woods. Beneath the beam of an ultra-violet (UV) lamp, the lichens of the forest come alive. The usual greens and greys of the lichen carpet are transformed into a sea of bright colours – blues, oranges and pinks start to dance before our eyes as chemicals in the lichens light up in the UV light.

Lichen light shows

Lichens that absorb UV light in this way are found not just in our woodlands, but in a variety of habitats, from mountain tops to coastal rocks; they can even appear right under our feet – on pavements. In fact, one of the best light-show lichens is *Cladonia squamosa*, which will grow on bare soil. It glows so vividly that it's hard to believe that it's natural.

Chris and Sally (top) inspect lichen nightlife under ultra-violet (UV) light. Fungi and lichens from many walks of life (below) glow in the dark as chemicals in their body light up in UV light.

Why lichens glow

Impressive though it is, the lichen light show is really an accidental side effect of the species' self-protective mechanisms. To defend themselves from potential harm – ranging from hungry snails to harsh sunlight – lichens produce a variety of chemicals called 'lichen substances'. It is these substances that absorb UV light and, in the process, cause lichens to glow. UV radiation from the sun is potentially damaging, as it can cause mutations in the cells of all species on earth and its effects are strong enough to kill any unprotected organism. As the UV levels on

earth were much higher c.500 million years ago, when lichens first evolved, the species developed a particularly effective chemical weaponry to withstand high levels of UV radiation.

Within the lichen home (see p.45), it is the fungal partner that provides a sunscreen, producing the protective substances that shield both the lichen itself and the algae within. This is one of the many ways in which the partners help each other out. The special relationship between the two can be likened to that of any good marriage, where responsibilities are shared and no single party is left to do all the work. The algae largely takes on the role of breadwinner, putting food on the table for all to enjoy, while the fungus plays the homemaker, providing a safe and secure shelter, protected from moisture loss and, crucially, free of UV radiation.

Nature's super sunscreens

In fact, lichens' remarkable capacity to withstand UV radiation has prompted scientists to study them in the hope of developing a new natural sunscreen, based on the very chemicals that are produced by the lichens themselves. Certain lichens, such as the golden hair lichen (*Teloschistes flavicans*), which grows in Antarctica where the ozone hole is largest, have evolved to survive far greater levels of UV radiation than anywhere else. This species has developed sunscreens that are strong enough to withstand extremely high levels of UV radiation – it is even capable of surviving the UV levels of outer space.

It is these 'super sunscreen' lichens that are being put to the test in an effort to develop an effective natural sun cream for human use; and we're now bringing these amazing lichen chemicals from the frozen wastes of Antarctica to sunnier climes around the world.

Cladonia squamosa *looks eerie enough in broad daylight but glows vivid white under the beam of a UV light.*

RAINFOREST LICHENS

You don't have to travel far to find a rainforest. Britain is well known for its rain, but for once this is good news and reveals a surprising story about what's right here on our doorstep. Water-soaked winds driven off the Atlantic Ocean drench our west coast. Some upland areas are subjected to more than 1.5m of rain, but this annual soaking has created the ideal conditions for one particularly magical and little-known habitat.

When you go into a wood and find lichens dripping from the boughs, or mosses carpeting the floor, you can start to piece the clues together. Their presence here is down to the warm, wet conditions, which are perfect for their growth, but there are more surprising clues to detect.

Some lichens that make a home in these damp conditions can also be used as a kind of wild 'rain gauge'. *Sticta fuliginosa*, for example, is mostly found in places that receive more than 200 days of rain a year, so it can be used as an indicator species (see p.73). It very clearly gives us a message about the amount of rain an area receives. As forests that receive such high rainfall are officially known as rainforests, it's proof that whenever you find *Sticta fuliginosa*, anywhere in the world, you're in a rainforest. No rain gauge necessary! So the British Isles are actually home to 'rainforests', a word that we more commonly associate with the far-flung forests of tropical lands. Yet this beguiling habitat can be found right down the western side of our country. Some extraordinary lichens flourish here and nowhere else. Other lichens grow in such great abundance in these precious woods that they make our temperate rainforests more important, in some ways, than the better-known rainforests of the Amazon.

Being able to identify this rainforest lichen not only tells you that you are somewhere pretty wet (and you should pack your waterproofs), but it also firmly signals that you're in one of Britain's most important woodlands and a 'rainforest' at that. So you really don't have to travel halfway round the world to say that you've visited a rainforest.

In one of our British rainforests in Snowdonia, North Wales, Sally inspects some rainforest species (below left). The map (below) highlights where the rather wet Sticta fuliginosa *grows – where we can find our 'rainforests'.*

STICTA FULIGINOSA

TODAY

LOOKING TO THE FUTURE

It's hard not to react when we see statistics suggesting that our native woodland plants are disappearing. It's true that some studies do show woodlands to be a relatively stable habitat, but nearly one in five forest flowers are either threatened with extinction, or heading that way; and some familiar plants, such as sanicle (*Sanicula europaea*), are declining. As these species disappear, other wild things move out of our forests, too. The pearl-bordered fritillary, for instance, feeds on nectar from woodland flowers, such as bugle (*Ajuga reptans*), while its caterpillars eat dog violet (*Viola riviniana*), but it has declined by 80 per cent since 1985. Woodland birds, also, are disappearing: since 1970, the wood warbler, willow tit and tree pipit have all declined by over 70 per cent. So, what's the answer?

Fresh light on old ground

As we discovered earlier, most woodland plants love light, despite growing in the shade of a forest (see p.81). Only a very few, such as sweet woodruff and the ghost orchid, thrive in deep shade (see pp.73, 76). Walk into any typical wood and you'll see that all the plants are growing along the tracks and rides, in glades and openings, anywhere in fact where there is a gap in the canopy that allows light to stream through and reach the ground. Let the light in and the plants come out!

Some of our forests, however, have become overgrown, as we no longer use them as we once did. In the past, huge amounts of timber were cut for building. Firewood was collected for heating and cooking; leaves were gathered to feed and bed-down animals; poles and branches were cut to make walls and fences, and to craft bows and arrows. Although few of us, perhaps, have strung an arrow recently, almost every farm and settlement would have continued to use the local woods for their needs, at least until the early twentieth century. Constant use of the forests meant that they were continuously changing, with some parts of woodland recently felled and others left to mature. Such 'diversity of management' fuelled a rich variety of wild things.

Times have changed. Today much of our woodland is fenced off and left unmanaged. As the trees mature, they grow crowded, and dense canopies shut out the light. As our forests become darker,

Woodland plants provide food and nectar for many species such as the pearl-bordered fritillary. The fate of both the forest plants and the species associated with them is closely linked and depends on how we manage our woodlands.

Reading the trees

Trees can tell us some remarkable things, largely because they take so long to grow and can live for hundreds, even thousands of years. Some, such as the oak, take up to 300 years to reach maturity, while others, such as yews, can endure much longer, sometimes for several thousand years. As they grow, their own history and that of the land around them becomes part of their shape and structure. We just have to read the clues in the trees.

Look at where they're growing.
Are your trees lined up in a hedgerow beside a road or lane, with big old specimen trees and smaller ones in-between? If so, you're probably looking at the very edge of what was once a forest (above). As this forest was cleared to make open fields, the trees at the edge were left to mark the boundary.

Look at how the trees are branching.
If lots of boughs or small trunks branch from the base of the trees, they're likely to have been coppiced in the past (below). This means that all the boughs were cut down for timber, and new branches were allowed to sprout from the base to be harvested again in a few years' time, once big enough.

Look at the trunks of the trees.
Are they all roughly similar in width? If so, it's likely that the woodland was once felled and that all the trees have since grown back together, much like a classroom full of children of roughly the same age and size who grow up together. Despite having been cleared, such woodland can be rich in wild things. In the example above, from near Caernarfon in North Wales, a very rare orchid, the sword-leaved helleborine (*Cephalanthera longifolia*), can sometimes be found.

so the woodland plants on the forest floor decline, and the wild things on which the forest depends move out. Should we aim to replicate the old ways and thin out woodland trees periodically? It would certainly help, although not all woodlands would need to be managed in this way all the time. Some forests would be better left to mature undisturbed, encouraging the growth of ancient trees dripping with mosses, liverworts and lichens (see pp.84–5).

Rich in use, rich in wild things

Diversity is the key to healthy woodland. The ideal would be for different types of woodland to be managed in different ways. Our woodlands today are all looking too much alike, a bit like our high streets with their replica identikit shops and loss of local character.

True, more woodland is now being established, whether newly planted or left to seed and regenerate naturally; and it is very much needed, as new growth helps to connect together the tiny fragments of woodland that remain in much of the British landscape.

But, rather than simply quantity, what we also need is better quality woodland – rich in use and rich in wild things.

A wild horse laps from a stream in the New Forest, Hampshire, southern England, where grazing animals help to keep the undergrowth down and the paths open, letting in the light.

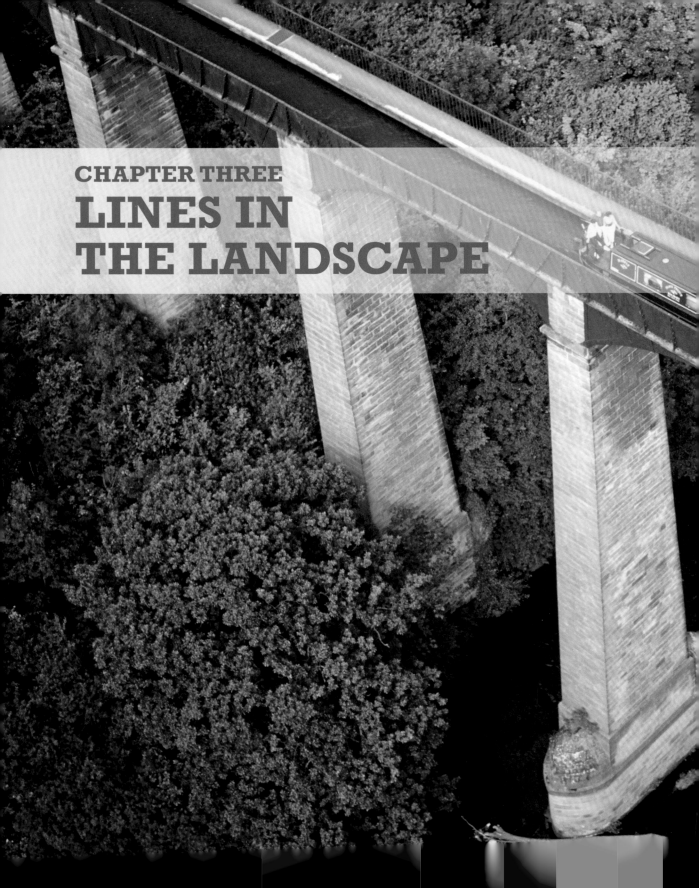

CHAPTER THREE
LINES IN
THE LANDSCAPE

PREVIOUS PAGE The Pontcysyllte Aqueduct, which opened in 1805, carries the Llangollen Canal 38m above the River Dee near Rhiwabon in Wales.

Every year, 34 million vehicles travel over 394,398km of road stretching across the British Isles. On our railways,16,513km of track carry more than 19,000 trains each day, ferrying both passengers and freight, while on British waterways 13 million people use about 3,540km of navigable canals every year.

ABOVE Canals provide routes by which a wide variety of plants can move through the country, both in the water and along the towpaths.

ABOVE CENTRE Crisscrossing road junctions witness a multitude of wild things coming and going, and offer valuable habitats along their verges.

With all this movement around the country, it's no wonder that some botanical hitch-hikers have taken the opportunity to thumb a lift: whether airborne in a railway carriage, such as Oxford ragwort (*Senecio squalidus*), or clinging to the tyres of a car, such as prickly lettuce (*Lactuca serriola*), they've benefited from a free ride to new places, sometimes travelling huge distances to put down roots in fresh soil (see pp.92–104, 106–107).

The rise in modern mobility over the past fifty years has clearly played a crucial role in the distribution of plants and other wild things, which have not only spread on the wheels of our vehicles, but also made new homes along the edges of our roads, canals and railways. With our vast transport network, we've carved out lines in the landscape, which have provided fresh new 'linear' habitats in which wild things can flourish. Today, more native flowering plants, at least 370 species in all, grow in linear homes than in any other, reflecting the rich variety of habitat types, ranging from grassy roadside verges to shaded country lanes, from railway tracks and embankments to canal towpaths. Many are incredibly important refuges for wild things, often providing substitutes for habitats that

have long since vanished from the surrounding countryside. Our roadside verges, for instance, are now awash with a riot of flowers and colour, offering an alternative habitat for the large numbers of meadows that have disappeared under the plough during the last century (see chapter 6). Country lane hedgerows, also, grow thick with berries and nesting sites, providing an excellent substitute for some of our vanished woodlands (see chapter 2).

Certain linear habitats, though, can seem harsh and inhospitable, such as dry railway clinker or bare, exposed motorways, yet various plants and other wild things have not only managed to move into these unfamiliar spaces, but even to flourish in their new homes …

ABOVE With miles of leafy habitats lining their busy tracks, railway lines provide long corridors along which plants can flourish and spread.

ROADS

For many of us, roads and motorways provide some of the quickest and easiest ways of moving around the British Isles. With almost every house, village, town and city now connected by a network of roads, plant seeds can also join us on our journeys and spread far afield. Some seeds stick to the tyres of cars for miles on end, while others get blown along the carriageways by passing vehicles (see pp.102–3). All sorts of new plants are now appearing along our roadsides, making them exciting places to chance across unexpected discoveries.

DANISH SCURVYGRASS

With Danish scurvygrass (*Cochlearia danica*), we've witnessed one of the most incredible histories in plant distribution over the past fifty years. It's a story of how nature will always find a way of coping and adapting, even when humans throw some pretty hostile things at it.

Danish scurvygrass (inset) grows on damp, sandy and gravelly spots beside the sea, such as here at Porth-y-post in Anglesey, Wales, where the soil remains wet all winter.

DANISH SCURVYGRASS
COCHLEARIA DANICA

1962

1994

TODAY

Before the 1980s, Danish scurvygrass counted as a seaside plant, growing mostly where it had always been found, right around the coast of Britain and parts of Ireland. Being small and early flowering, usually in March, it was largely overlooked. Botanists didn't really take much notice of it, as there were far more interesting species to discover. Now, though, Danish scurvygrass cannot be ignored – it has penetrated to the very heart of rural England and become one of the fastest-spreading British plants of the last half-century. Drive along any major roads in most parts of the country during March and April and you'll notice ribbons of pale pinkish-white flowers flourishing along verges and central reservations.

This sequence of maps spanning the past fifty years shows the rapid spread of Danish scurvygrass along our road network, stretching from its home on the coast to the very heart of the British Isles.

On the scurvygrass trail

When and why did this coast-hugging plant move inland? Fifty years ago, Danish scurvygrass was first noticed straying further inshore at a scattering of mainland sites. These were mostly around Cheshire in western central England, where underground deposits of rock salt were being mined; and in southeast England, where the plant appeared on the rocky clinker of some railway tracks, although it would spread no further along the railroad.

ABOVE *When a stretch of the M6 motorway was closed for maintenance, Chris (inset) got the chance to take a closer look at the carpet of Danish scurvygrass now covering long stretches of one of our busiest motorways.*

OPPOSITE *Mapping Danish scurvygrass (insets) at the 2km-square scale in some parts of the British Isles has revealed a living road map. The network of roads radiating out from Norwich (2) are especially clear, as are the M6 heading north towards Scotland (1), and the M5 towards southwest England (4). London, though, appears as a blank space inside the M25 (3). To find out why, turn to p.101.*

Onto the motorways

Then in 1980 a patch of Danish scurvygrass was spotted for the first time on the A11 in Suffolk. Within a few years, more stretches were reported along the A45 in Cambridgeshire and it subsequently appeared on motorways in Kent and Surrey. Soon, the records started coming in thick and fast from many different parts of the country. This plant was on the move and spreading quickly; in fact, it seemed to be actually advancing through the road network, along miles and miles of it. By the mid 1990s, the A14 and M6 could be made out as a curved line of dots on the plant's distribution map; then the M5 emerged as another distinctive line of dots on the map (see p.93).

Today, the spread of Danish scurvygrass along our motorways and roads has been so immense that it's difficult to make out any particular roads on the national 10km-square distribution maps but, if we look at the more in-depth 2km-square maps (see opposite), a clearer picture emerges. In East Anglia, for example, mapping at the closer level has revealed an astonishing pattern of Danish scurvygrass running along the major roads as they radiate out from Norwich in eastern England and onto the M6, heading north towards Scotland. Similarly, a ring of Danish scurvygrass can be traced around London, faithfully following the M25 motorway.

DANISH SCURVYGRASS
COCHLEARIA DANICA

A CLOSER LOOK AT DANISH
SCURVYGRASS IN SOME PARTS
OF THE BRITISH ISLES: 2KM SCALE

- The trail to Scotland
- The Norwich network
- Inside the M25 motorway
- Heading southwest on the
  M5 motorway

TODAY

The plant is now found not only on the central reservations, but also along the verges of major roads – in fact, any spot with bare soil that is wet in winter might end up covered in Danish scurvygrass. Colonies have now joined together so that, on some stretches of road, entire undulating ribbons of Danish scurvygrass can be seen for miles.

Exactly how the distribution maps for this plant had changed so dramatically during the 1980s and 1990s became an intriguing puzzle. Why on earth was this coastal plant making inroads into the British Isles so quickly?

Not just for fish and chips

The answer lies in salt. Since the 1960s, salt has been spread onto the surface of roads in winter to help prevent the formation of ice and to reduce the build-up of snow. At least 2 million tonnes of it, mostly from rock salt mines in Cheshire, are applied to British roads each year at a cost of more than £150 million.

How does salt help to melt snow? Common salt (sodium chloride), lowers the point at which water freezes and also lowers the melting point, causing snow to melt faster. The more salt that is applied, the more the freezing and melting points will drop. Theoretically, it would take 17 tonnes of salt to melt a 2.5cm layer of ice on a 1.5km stretch of single carriageway, which is obviously impossible and not actually the aim at all. Salt is spread on roads to prevent ice and snow from freezing to the road surface in the first place, and it takes just 227kg of the mineral to achieve this.

Sea salt up-close – a coloured scanning electron micrograph showing the crystalline structure of this common mineral. Like pure table salt, sea salt consists mainly of sodium chloride, but also contains traces of other elements.

Turning roadside into seaside

By applying huge amounts of salt onto our roads every winter, we've created thousands of miles of perfect habitat for Danish scurvygrass. Thinking back to the coast where it came from, we can see that it prefers a very specific micro-habitat with few competitors: it thrives in open patches of shallow soil, preferably ones that are very wet in winter and heavily doused with salt spray from the sea, which sounds a little like a typical roadside edge after a winter splash of salt. When salt is spread on roads, three things happen:

1 *Large amounts land directly on the edge of the road.*
2 *Rain and melting snow eventually wash all the salt onto the edge.*
3 *Passing vehicles splash a great deal of salt onto the roadside.*

What all this means is that a huge amount of salt finds its way onto the verge and central reservation of our roads. Of the 2 million tonnes applied to our roads every year, almost all of it reaches these areas eventually.

Salt burn

Any salt sprayed onto a road tends to 'burn', or scorch, the vegetation on the edge of the road, along which a bare patch usually develops where most plants just can't cope with that level of salt. In fact, 83 per cent of wild plants in the British Isles cannot tolerate any salt at all, as it's absolutely toxic for them. So this bare patch, which is wet, open and usually filled with shallow soil, replicates perfectly the exact micro-niche along the sea coast where Danish scurvygrass thrives in its natural habitat. Once this seaside plant had found its way to the salty roadside, it just romped away.

All the salt used to keep our snow-bound roads safe ends up on the verges, either thrown by passing snow ploughs, or churned up with the melting snow and ice.

LINES IN THE LANDSCAPE

How does Danish scurvygrass survive the effects of salt?

Many of us might love it on our fish and chips but, for most wild things, too much salt is toxic. Yet this tough little plant can take all the salt you can chuck at it. The secret of its success, which is hidden in its name, is revealed by this experiment.

The equipment
1 x sandy beach
1 x fluorescence imaging camera
1 x Danish scurvygrass leaf
1 x crane's-bill leaf
1 x bottle of seawater
2 x ice creams

There's no better way to enjoy a day by the seaside than with an ice cream and a dollop of science. Danish scurvygrass has a secret biological trick that helps it to shrug off the effects of salt. With a bottle of seawater and our Land Rover laboratory, the *Wild Things* team set out to investigate how the plant copes with salt.

The method
A leaf of Danish scurvygrass and one of crane's-bill (*Geranium* sp.) were used for comparison. Both were placed in small test tubes filled with fresh seawater and then put in a special black box of tricks: a fluorescence imaging camera that captures real-time processes in live cells. The camera was switched on and the team waited for the show to begin. In the fluorescent light, it was possible to see how well the chlorophyll was working within the plant's cells. A green light meant that the leaf was alive and well, while a red light indicated that it was dying.

As the two leaves soaked up the seawater, the camera showed the crane's-bill turn quickly from green to red. When salty seawater entered the leaf, it could not cope with the salt, which upset the balance inside its cells and, within just a few minutes, the entire leaf had turned red. Beside it, though, Danish scurvygrass remained green, quite unaffected by the seawater. Somehow this coastal plant is able to fend off the damaging effects of salt

Chris and Trevor set up a beach laboratory in the back of the Land Rover and put crane's-bill and scurvygrass leaves to the test.

The two leaves were soaked in sea water (far left) and put under the fluorescence camera (left). The crane's-bill leaf (below left) quickly turned from green to red as the salt destroyed its cells (bottom), but Danish scurvygrass (below right) stayed green and healthy.

and carry on living as if nothing's bothering it at all. For Danish scurvygrass, it was just a perfectly normal day at the seaside!

THE SCIENCE

What smart survival trick enables Danish scurvygrass to tolerate the effects of salt? The camera revealed the answer in stages. As seawater was soaked up by the leaves, salt entered their cells. In a non-salt-tolerant plant, such as crane's-bill, the mineral upset the delicate balance within its cells, prompting the release of free radicals, which are highly reactive chemicals, quite as disruptive as they sound. Like rioting anarchists, they caused further damage, preventing the crane's-bill's chlorophyll from working properly. Without functioning chlorophyll, a plant simply cannot survive, as chlorophyll is the powerhouse of every plant and the site of photosynthesis – the incredible process whereby energy from sunlight is used to create glucose sugar from nothing more than carbon dioxide and water (see p.43). The sugar produced during photosynthesis provides the energy source for the whole plant, without which it cannot survive.

When the sun is shining and photosynthesis is ticking along nicely, most of the sunlight is absorbed and used by a plant's chlorophyll, but if the chlorophyll is damaged, photosynthesis starts shutting down, which is what happened to the crane's-bill when it was soaked in salt. Although its wasted light energy couldn't be seen by the naked eye, the fluorescence camera revealed it as red light, indicating a poorly functioning plant.

Danish scurvygrass, by contrast, is a halophyte, or salt plant, well adapted to saline conditions, such as salt marshes. Crucially, it has evolved a secret weapon to combat the free radicals provoked by salt – its leaves are packed full of vitamin C, an antioxidant that neutralizes the effect of free radicals, stopping their damaging reactions dead in their tracks.

The plant's common name hints at the vitamin C connection, as scurvy is a disease caused by a lack of vitamin C. Before diet was properly understood, sea-bound sailors were particularly prone to scurvy, as they endured long journeys without a healthy quota of fruit and vegetables, which are rich in vitamin C. On coming ashore, sailors would collect scurvygrass leaves along the coast to combat the effects of the disease.

CABBAGES ON THE COAST

Danish scurvygrass is a member of the cabbage or Brassicaceae family. The same biochemical mechanism that allows this species to thrive in heavy salt enables many others in the family to do the same. Along with Danish scurvygrass, cabbage species are packed with vitamin C, which acts as an antioxidant, neutralizing potentially damaging agents in a living organism. It was formerly eaten by sailors to prevent scurvy at sea (see pp. 98–9).

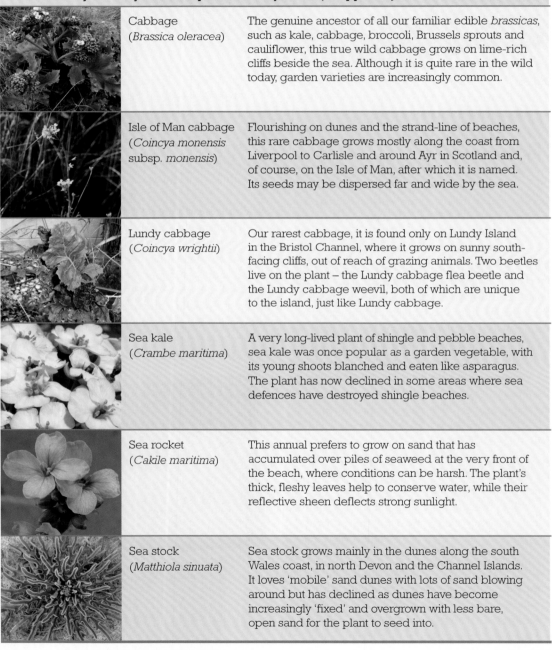

	Cabbage (*Brassica oleracea*)	The genuine ancestor of all our familiar edible *brassicas*, such as kale, cabbage, broccoli, Brussels sprouts and cauliflower, this true wild cabbage grows on lime-rich cliffs beside the sea. Although it is quite rare in the wild today, garden varieties are increasingly common.
	Isle of Man cabbage (*Coincya monensis* subsp. *monensis*)	Flourishing on dunes and the strand-line of beaches, this rare cabbage grows mostly along the coast from Liverpool to Carlisle and around Ayr in Scotland and, of course, on the Isle of Man, after which it is named. Its seeds may be dispersed far and wide by the sea.
	Lundy cabbage (*Coincya wrightii*)	Our rarest cabbage, it is found only on Lundy Island in the Bristol Channel, where it grows on sunny south-facing cliffs, out of reach of grazing animals. Two beetles live on the plant – the Lundy cabbage flea beetle and the Lundy cabbage weevil, both of which are unique to the island, just like Lundy cabbage.
	Sea kale (*Crambe maritima*)	A very long-lived plant of shingle and pebble beaches, sea kale was once popular as a garden vegetable, with its young shoots blanched and eaten like asparagus. The plant has now declined in some areas where sea defences have destroyed shingle beaches.
	Sea rocket (*Cakile maritima*)	This annual prefers to grow on sand that has accumulated over piles of seaweed at the very front of the beach, where conditions can be harsh. The plant's thick, fleshy leaves help to conserve water, while their reflective sheen deflects strong sunlight.
	Sea stock (*Matthiola sinuata*)	Sea stock grows mainly in the dunes along the south Wales coast, in north Devon and the Channel Islands. It loves 'mobile' sand dunes with lots of sand blowing around but has declined as dunes have become increasingly 'fixed' and overgrown with less bare, open sand for the plant to seed into.

ROADSIDE CRESS

Like the best of travellers, hoary cress (*Lepidium draba*), a member of the cabbage family, has utilized all sorts of transport to get around (right). It appears to have stowed away on a boat, perhaps from southern Europe or Asia where it originates, and then turned up at the port of Swansea in Wales in 1802. From there, it moved onto the railways, spreading along dry clinker and embankments, then hopped onto the roads, where it particularly liked disturbed and freshly turned soil. Today, hoary cress is also found more widely on disturbed soil in fields, on waste ground and beside the seaside, but you're still most likely to see it as a white froth on a roadside verge.

A puzzle solved

Now that it's clear why Danish scurvygrass spreads along our major road networks, we can perhaps explain why, in some instances, it doesn't. Turning back to the 2km-square map (see p.95), what's particularly curious is the relative lack of Danish scurvygrass in central London, which you'd expect to be teeming with the plant, particularly since the capital lies at the hub of a busy road network encircled by the M25 motorway. Once inside the M25, though, the plant trail simply peters out. A clue to the anomaly lies in the fact that London is an urban heat island, built of brick, stone, steel, concrete and other materials that just absorb and hold on to heat, reducing the need for salt on snow-bound roads. Even in winter, this urban heat effect is enough to lessen the use of salt in London, which explains why Danish scurvygrass shrinks inside the capital.

The plant trail in Ireland throws up another anomaly. A glance at the Irish map and you'll notice that some Danish scurvygrass seems to be growing on inland roads in Northern Ireland but very little appears in the Republic of Ireland (see p.93), presumably because in the Republic there is no statutory obligation to apply salt to winter roads. The lack of regular salt-spreading, combined with our milder climate and a growing tendency to use grit instead, suggests that less salt is being used in the Republic than anywhere else in the British Isles – and less salt means less Danish scurvygrass.

Is Danish scurvygrass the fastest-travelling plant?

An acquired taste for salt might explain why Danish scurvygrass has spread along our roadside verges (see pp.98–9), but does not tell us how this seaside plant has managed to move so rapidly from the coast to the hub of our busy road network. This experiment reveals exactly how.

The equipment
1 x fast car
1 x very experienced driver
1 x phantom camera to record
   slow-motion footage
1 x very large indoor area
1000s of tiny polystyrene balls

The method
To reveal this plant's remarkable ability to travel across the country, the *Wild Things* team set up an experiment that involved re-creating a little piece of the M6 motorway inside Birmingham's National Exhibition Centre (NEC). Into this controlled environment was added a fast car, a slow-motion camera and some polystyrene balls.

Danish scurvygrass seeds are tiny, no more than 1mm long. In order to see the whirlwind effect that a passing car would have on the lightweight seeds, some slightly larger but equally light polystyrene balls, painted in fluorescent yellow, were used as an alternative to the seeds. Inside the controlled NEC, these 'seedballs' were spread out on the ground and left undisturbed so that only the effect of the car, travelling at motorway speed, could be recorded. It all sounds simple enough. The only slight snag was that the driver had just a short stretch of 240m within which to reach a top speed of 112.5km per hour; and then only 70m in which to stop.

Danish scurvygrass can produce thousands of tiny seeds (below left) each no more than 1mm long. For the experiment, some larger but equally light polystyrene balls (left) were spread on the ground inside Birmingham's National Exhibition Centre. With some fast precision driving, our car demonstrated how such 'seedballs' can be swept along our roads (below).

THE SCIENCE

The slow-motion camera showed how the aerodynamics of a speeding car crucially help the spread of Danish scurvygrass. First, the flow of air around the tyres lifts seeds from the ground. The lightweight seeds are then suspended in mid-air, which is when the real magic occurs: in the wake of a passing car, a spinning column of air develops, like a mini-tornado. This whirlwind raises the already airborne seeds even higher, until they're eventually dragged along by the car's backdraft. The greater the speed of the vehicle, the greater the whirlwind created.

Quite simply, the fast lane of a motorway creates the perfect storm for the spread of Danish scurvygrass. Out there on our motorways and major roads, the whirlwind effect occurs thousands of times a day. All those millions of scurvygrass seeds are hitching a ride on the backdraft of our cars, which is why Danish scurvygrass is the fastest-travelling plant in the British Isles today.

As the car speeds by, its tyres throw the seedballs into the air (below left). In the wake of the car, mini-tornadoes lift the balls even higher (below right), sweeping them along. As a result, miles of roadside are carpeted with a ribbon of white Danish scurvygrass each spring (above).

Like Danish scurvygrass, thrift is another seaside plant that has appeared on our salty roadside verges. Its seeds are twice the size of Danish scurvygrass, though, which is probably why it has not spread very far.

More warmth, less salt

Just as we've created a new habitat for Danish scurvygrass, we could as easily bring it all to an end. If we switch to alternative de-icers, for instance, Danish scurvygrass could easily retreat. We might well try other de-icers, as the rock salt that we currently use, though cheap, washes off easily and is not that effective in extremely cold conditions. Alternatives, such as potassium and magnesium chloride, calcium magnesium acetate (CMA) from limestone, and various other organic substances are all being investigated. If they reduce or even replace the use of salt, Danish scurvygrass could well disappear from our roadsides just as quickly as it arrived. If, at the same time, winters become warmer and wetter, then even less salt will end up on our roads, shrinking the plant's salty habitat even further.

A seaside community along the verge

We have developed an extensive roadside habitat for our coastal plants in the British Isles. Along thousands of miles of verges, the salt, wind and spray have created conditions identical to parts of the coast, allowing seaside plants to colonize far inland. Apart from Danish scurvygrass, several other coastal species have populated our roadsides, though none quite as quickly nor as spectacularly as Danish scurvygrass. Reflexed saltmarsh grass (*Puccinellia distans*), grass-leaved orache (*Atriplex littoralis*) and buck's-horn plantain (*Plantago coronopus*) all add to a wonderful seaside community along our verges. It almost makes you want to get your deckchairs out by the side of the road. Other species, such as thrift (*Armeria maritima*) and sea aster (*Aster tripolium*), have appeared in a few places but failed to spread far. Still others, including dittander (*Lepidium latifolium*) and lesser sea-spurrey (*Spergularia marina*), seem to be increasing rapidly on the roads in many parts of the British Isles. Could one of them be the Danish scurvygrass of the future? Quite possibly, as in this new and dynamic habitat along our roads, plants are constantly changing.

FLOWERING TIMES												
	J	F	M	A	M	J	J	A	S	O	N	D
Danish scurvygrass	✿	✿	✿	✿	✿	✿	✿	✿	✿	✿	✿	✿

SUMMER CYPRESS

Although summer cypress (*Bassia scoparia*) is closely related to beetroot and spinach, its narrow but dense branching leaves make it look like a dwarf conifer, hence its common name cypress, after the cypress conifer family (*Cupressaceae*). It is grown in gardens for its crowning glory in the autumn when its leaves turn from pink to red and yellow, until the whole bush becomes a flaming beacon, which explains its other common name – burning bush.

Summer cypress is a plant that certainly knows how to get about. It was first recorded growing in the wild in Surrey, southeast England, in around 1866, but it remained rare until 1994, when it was spotted on the verge of the M18 motorway near Thorne in Yorkshire, northern England. Its spread was then rapid and dramatic. More plants were seen in 1995 and by 1997 it was noticed along the A63 west of Hull and on the A1033 east of Hull in northern England. Today the plant grows all around the Humber Estuary in northern

ABOVE *The fine feathery foliage of summer cypress resembles a conifer.*

BELOW *The recent spread of summer cypress along our roads is clear to see from these two maps.*

SUMMER CYPRESS
BASSIA SCOPARIA

1962

TODAY

England. Since 2002, it's also taken off further south, especially on the M5 motorway and on the A34 and A303 in Hampshire.

Summer cypress has an unusual and brilliant way of getting around – in fact, it's our version of American tumbleweed, such as Russian thistle (*Salsola tragus*), often seen in Western movies rolling around in the dust of desolate frontier towns. In much the same way, summer cypress is blown around after it dies at the end of each year, when its rounded bushy top breaks away from the soil. Once detached, the wispy top is easily swept up by the backdraft of passing cars, and sent flying, bouncing, cart-wheeling and rolling along the verges, scattering seeds as it goes. It's been observed travelling at over 16km per hour – not bad for a plant. As it tumbles, the tiny 1mm-wide seeds are knocked out of their pods and find new places to grow.

Summer cypress, also known as burning bush, turns bright pink and yellow in autumn as the plant dies. Once dead, it becomes detached from its roots and tumbles along the ground, scattering seed as it goes. In Japan, these seeds are eaten as a delicacy called tonburi, *or land caviar.*

PRICKLY LETTUCE

Although prickly lettuce (*Lactuca serriola*) is closely related to our ordinary edible lettuce (*L. sativa*), its prickly leaves and bitter taste mean that you're far better off sticking to little gems or icebergs. It's been around for a very long time, since at least 1632, when it was first recorded in the wild. The plant has only spread rapidly in the late twentieth century, however. Its recent increase was monitored in a national survey, which found that the plant was almost three times more commonly recorded in 2004 than it had been seventeen years earlier.

Prickly lettuce is one of the first species to colonize the bare soil alongside newly constructed roads, as its small light seed gets carried along on vehicle tyres. It also seems to prefer the warmer climates of recent years, since it increased in abundance after the famous hot summer and drought of 1976, so perhaps it's now spreading in response to climate change.

It's certainly a plant that knows where it's going. As the stem grows, the leaves twist round to point upwards, thereby avoiding direct sunlight. They also turn roughly east and west, ensuring that only their narrow edges will face the sun in the midday heat, which helps to reduce water loss. It's just in the early morning and late afternoon that the plant's leaves face the sun directly as it rises in the east and sets in the west. If you're lost and need a compass, try prickly lettuce, which is otherwise known as the compass plant.

PRICKLY LETTUCE
LACTUCA SERRIOLA

1962

TODAY

ABOVE *The rapid spread of prickly lettuce in the last fifty years is clearly illustrated by the solid mass of dots (above right). Although now widespread on roads in much of England, it's still uncommon in the west and Scotland.*

LEFT *Tall plants of prickly lettuce flower on the edge of the A5 near Shrewsbury, Shropshire. The plant's leaves (inset) orientate themselves vertically and point east—west, to avoid the harsh midday sun and to minimize water loss.*

CITY LICHENS

Our congested, polluted cities often seem harsh and inhospitable, shrouded in urban dust and car fumes, which can hardly be healthy for most wild things. Lichens, especially, are generally sensitive to pollution because they lack the protective outer skin, known as a cuticle, which most plants rely on to prevent any contact between nasties in the atmosphere and their precious cells within. In addition, lichens have no roots like most other plants (see p.45). Instead, they take whatever they need to survive by absorbing it over their entire surface area, which makes them especially susceptible to air- and rainwater-borne pollutants, such as car exhaust fumes.

Not all lichens are sensitive to pollution to the same degree, however. Some can be quite tolerant of pollutants that others

After searching hard, Sally spots the tough little lichen Lecanora conizaeoides *(below) flourishing deep within the cracks and crannies of old gravestones (bottom).*

absolutely can't stand. This is because individual species have, over time, acquired their own unique armoury with which to overcome any dangerous situations in which they might find themselves. As a result, some species have learnt to tolerate particular poisons that others simply could not survive.

An 'acid raincoat'

Lecanora conizaeoides is an excellent example of a lichen that did just that. Living in the mountain pine bogs of central Europe, it got used to extremely acidic conditions and developed a variety of ways in which to shield itself from acid. One such mechanism involved the production of some hydrophobic or water-hating crystals (made from fumarprotocetraric acid). The lichen wore these crystals like a coat, which prevented the acidic water in the bogs from soaking through to its cells. This hardy little *Lecanora*, though tough as old boots, was slow to develop and therefore couldn't compete with lichens growing outside the bogs, but it was able to thrive in these acidic conditions where few other lichens could survive. It grew in bogs and nowhere else, becoming known as one of Europe's rarest lichens, until …

During the nineteenth century, the Industrial Revolution caused much coal to be burnt in our cities, releasing vast amounts of sulphur into the air. Combining with oxygen, this sulphur then dissolved into water to produce what we know today as acid rain. As the acid rained down from the skies on our cities, the surfaces on which lichens grew – ranging from tree trunks to stone walls and pavements – became more

Morning dawns on a city smothered in a haze of air pollution, created by exhaust fumes and urban dust.

and more acidic. As a result, the lichens that had once commonly lived in such places could no longer stand the acidic conditions and gradually became rarer sights.

Streetwise *Lecanora*

Cue *Lecanora conizaeoides*. It was as though it had been waiting its whole life for this moment. The acidic conditions that were now present in many of Europe's cities were ideal for this lichen with its special raincoat shield. Very quickly it spread from the pine bogs to cover vast swathes of our cities, applying itself like a paint to urban walls, trees and buildings – it covered virtually every surface. Though this situation was great for *Lecanora*, it was not so good for all the lichens that had gone before, as its presence indicated that we'd created conditions that were unsuitable for many life forms.

Listening to lichens

After the Great Smog in 1952, when a dense, smoke-filled fog brought London to a standstill, the British government passed the Clean Air Acts of 1956 and 1968. Under their rules, smoky fuels, such as coal, could no longer be burnt in our cities, making acid rain a thing of the past. Just as quickly as it had appeared, the little *Lecanora* started retreating back to its pine bogs.

Today, thanks to the changes we made in the 1950s, acid rain is no longer a problem in our cities. Unfortunately, this doesn't mean that we are pollution-free and we now face different problems, with pollutants such as nitrates causing havoc in natural systems. Just as before, some lichens fare better than others in these conditions.

As we better understand the sensitivity of certain lichens to particular pollutants, our use of the species as pollutant indicators becomes more and more effective. By listening to lichens, we are able to predict where pollutants are having an impact on our environment, which gives us a chance to act before they move further down the food chain and affect larger organisms, such as bugs, birds and even ourselves.

RAILWAYS

Our railway network stretches across the country in long lines of unbroken and often undisturbed tracts of land, providing ideal spaces in which wild things can thrive and spread. Train passengers, too, have played an important part in the dispersal of seed as they climb in and out of carriages at platforms up and down the country.

RAILWAY RAGWORTS

The dramatic spread of Oxford ragwort in the last fifty years shows how a plant can use the railways to get around initially and then fan out into suitable habitats all over the country.

On the volcanic slopes of Mount Etna on the island of Sicily in Italy, two species of ragwort grow, *Senecio aethnensis* and *Senecio chrysanthemifolius*. On the whole, the first prefers conditions at high altitude, while the second is happier lower down the slopes, but some plants of both species gravitate towards the middle ground – halfway up and halfway down, much like the Grand Old Duke of York's 'ten thousand men' in the popular nursery rhyme.

At this halfway point, the stage is set for evolution. It is here in the so-called 'hybrid zone' that the two ragworts have interacted and cross-bred for centuries, producing varied hybrids.

A new chapter in the ragwort's history opened in the late seventeenth century, when some travellers on the Grand Tour collected seeds of the Sicilian hybrids and brought them back to Oxford Botanic Garden, where the hybrid was recorded growing in 1690. Hybrid plants are often genetically unstable, as their new combinations of genes – one set from each parent – are not comfortable with each other at first and need time to settle down. Over the next 100 years, the hybrid ragworts grew and reproduced in Oxford Botanic Garden, repeatedly crossing between themselves and generating plants with new mixtures of genes. Removed from their hot, dry, volcanic home in Sicily and now growing in cool, wet Oxford, new strains evolved and, as the genes were continually swapped around between the different ragworts, some varieties did better than others – evolution was underway. The ragworts that adjusted best to their new Oxford climate thrived, settled down and produced seed, which in turn generated more offspring; whereas the ragworts that continued to struggle in the cooler conditions failed to multiply. Eventually, a hybrid ragwort emerged that loved the British climate. It had taken the best and most vigorous bits from its Sicilian parents but was more suited to Oxford's cool, wet climate. A new species was born.

Like all flowers of the daisy family (Asteraceae), those of Oxford ragwort are composed of many tiny flowers, or florets, crowded together on a flat disk. Most of the florets have short petals, but sometimes one on the edge of the disk produces a particularly long petal, which forms one ray of the main flower head.

Just the ticket

Before long, in 1792, the new ragwort escaped from Oxford Botanic Garden and started popping up all over the local walls. The energetic citizen quickly spread its seed and colonized the city, after which it was soon named. Over the next fifty years, naturalists collected its seed to grow in other botanic gardens and, as a result, the plant appeared in a few more places around the British Isles. The story then took a dramatic turn when, in about 1879, the ragwort found its way onto Oxford's railway station. Three factors in its biology then came into play:

1   *It produces abundant seeds – in fact, a mature Oxford ragwort can generate about 10,000 seeds in a year.*

2   *Each seed is carried in the air by a miniature parachute – a tuft of fine white hairs that catch the slightest breeze.*

3   *It has not lost its preference – inherited from its original forebears on Mount Etna – for well-drained rocky places.*

These were the perfect traits for what turned out to be an astonishing spread of Oxford ragwort along the railways. The clinker and ballast used under the rails provided an imitation of the well-drained rocky volcanic slopes of its Sicilian homeland. Truly vast amounts of seed were produced, enabling the ragwort to spread rapidly. Wafted, carried and blown along by the trains, its tiny seed parachutes travelled for miles. In this way, Oxford ragwort was transported around the British Isles wherever the railways went. It reached northern England just a few years later, progressing to the central belt of Scotland in the mid 1950s. Today Oxford ragwort is ubiquitous. It thrives in practically every village, town and city in the British Isles, growing in pavement cracks, on walls, along roadsides, on waste ground, beside canals and anywhere and everywhere with a well-drained spot. From the volcanic slopes of Mount Etna, it has journeyed to almost the whole of Britain and Ireland.

Oxford ragwort can be seen flowering all around our towns, cities and villages in early spring. It especially likes well-drained spots that mimic the rocky volcanic slopes of its ancestors, such as railway stations, waste ground, walls and pavements.

Evolution, evolution, evolution

There's a final twist to the tale of Oxford ragwort. Once at large in the British countryside at the turn of the century, this Casanova of the railways continued its promiscuous liaisons with the local weeds. In 1925 in northern Wales, it met up with one of our commonest weeds, groundsel (*Senecio vulgaris*), and crossed with it to produce an entirely new species, Welsh groundsel (*Senecio cambrensis*). A few decades later in 1979 Oxford ragwort crossed again with groundsel, on this occasion near a railway station in York, producing another species, York groundsel (*Senecio eboracensis*).

Both Welsh and York groundsel are entirely new species, two of only six that have been documented in the last 100 years. Clearly, both are evidence of complex genetic mechanisms of evolution at work – a fact that has sparked off some heated debate, which has focused especially on York groundsel. Following examination of its DNA from pressed herbarium specimens, it was formally named a newly evolved species in

2003 and declared as proof of Charles Darwin's theory of evolution. An article in *The Times* online of 20 February 2003 claimed the discovery showed that 'Darwin was right and the creationists are wrong…'. This was, of course, rather taken as it was intended and creationists (who believe that the universe was created by God) were apoplectic. Claims and counter-claims, arguments and counter-arguments followed in quick succession. Each volley seemed to do nothing but ratchet up the hysteria. One religious Internet forum (www.christianforums.com) devotes seven pages of debate to the subject, including the wonderful line, 'More evolutionist nonsense. Someone somewhere may have been smoking weed, but I doubt if they found a newly evolved weed.'

In the meantime, while the arguments raged, York groundsel met an untimely end. Just as it had begun to spread, the new species was eradicated by an over-zealous campaign of herbicidal street-cleaning undertaken by the City of York Council. Seventeen years after its discovery, it was declared extinct in the wild in 2000.

ABOVE LEFT Native groundsel, a very common weed of cultivated and disturbed soil, has crossed more than once with Oxford ragwort, producing both York and Welsh groundsel in the twentieth century.

ABOVE RIGHT One product of the cross between Oxford ragwort and native groundsel was the entirely new species, Welsh groundsel.

HITCHING A FREE RIDE

Famously, Oxford ragwort's feathery seed parachutes sometimes literally took a ride on the early trains of the period (right). In 1927 the eminent botanist George Druce reported in *The Flora of Oxfordshire* that he'd actually observed one such seed take a journey by rail: 'I have seen them enter a railway-carriage window near Oxford and remain suspended in the air in the compartment until they found an exit at Tilehurst.' Remarkably for a seed, it had spread 65km in just forty minutes!

WILD WORLDS

Wonderful waterbears

Did you know that we have bears living among us? Known as waterbears or, more technically, as tardigrades, they are some of our toughest wild things.

Such miniature animals, or 'micro-fauna', are among the most important organisms to humans, as they recycle our waste and decompose dead matter making sure that our world is kept clean and that nutrients are made available for new growth. But what thanks do they get? None at all, as they're probably the least known and least liked group of any organism – nematode worms, micro-arthropods, ciliates and flagellates. Who's ever heard of them?

Take a simple sample from your garden – a thimbleful of mulch from a mossy flowerbed, a couple of decaying leaves or lichen-covered twigs. Mix them with water and pop a single

Sally collects some garden mulch (top right) for microscopic analysis with Trevor and Chris (centre right). In their waking, hydrated state, waterbears (below) are cuddly looking creatures that amble slowly through their watery habitats, clambering over obstacles in search of algae and other forms of food.

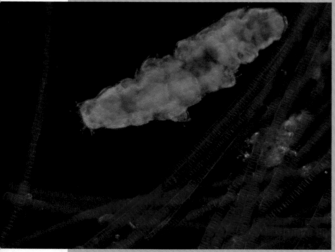

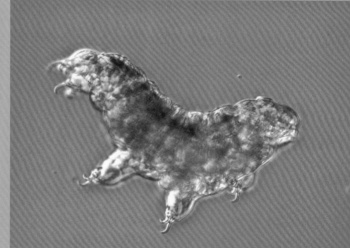

drop of the solution onto a microscope slide. Under magnification, you'll be astounded by the busy scenes that play out before your eyes. Tiny worms wrestle with shape-shifting amoebas; frustrated flagellates use their whip-like tails to frantically manoeuvre seemingly boulder-sized soil granules; and busy ciliates accidentally bump into everyone, like the local gossip. You can't fail to be entertained, but the best is yet to come!

Seemingly giant lumbering bears enter the scene, complete with a head and four pairs of legs. They amble around looking somehow wise and regal, munching on algae and using their squat legs to clamber over the other mini-beasts. These waterbears are the tardigrades (literally, 'slow-walkers') and not only do they look like the most tremendous of creatures, but they have some fantastic abilities too.

Shape-shifting survivors

Living in damp places, tardigrades have grown used to ambling around in water. If conditions dry up, though, they don't just curl up and die but do something really quite extraordinary – they enter a state of cryptobiosis (hidden life), a form of hibernation. By losing up to 90 per cent of

the water in their bodies and replacing it with sugars, tardigrades can retract their legs and head, turning themselves into a tough little cylinder that we call a tun.

In their dehydrated, tun-like state, tardigrades are able to survive a variety of extreme conditions, from droughts to temperatures as high as 151°C and as low as −237°C. They have even been sent into outer space in this state and returned perfectly unharmed!

Waterbears can survive in their tun-like state for hundreds of years, waiting for conditions to improve. When normality returns, the tardigrades – having possibly just endured anything from a volcanic explosion to an atomic bomb – very quickly re-emerge and get back to their mundane life, as though nothing in the least bit extraordinary has happened.

The sequence of microscopic images (below) show the tardigrade in its dehydrated, hibernated state (left) with all its appendages retracted in the form of a barrel-like 'tun'. Re-emerging from its tun state (right), the tardigrade starts to take on its waking form again, with its squat head and legs poking out from beneath its swollen body as it fills up with water once more.

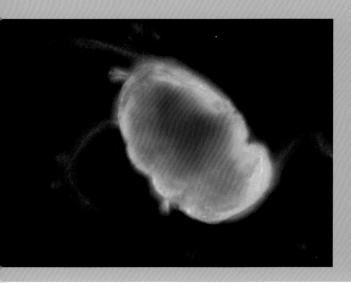
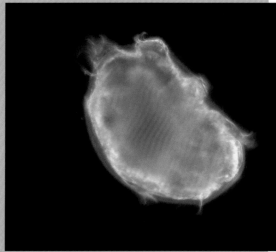

CANALS AND RIVERS

Fuelled by the demands of the Industrial Revolution, the massive development of the canal network during the eighteenth century opened up many new opportunities for plants and wildlife to move through the British Isles. Today, rivers and canals provide distinct lines in the landscape, resulting in the unexpected spread of many wild things.

TOWPATH BEGGARTICKS

The distribution map for beggarticks (*Bidens frondosa*) is one of the few that clearly reveals part of the British canal network along which this plant has spread. A member of the daisy family, beggarticks comes from North and South America and was first cultivated in British gardens in around 1710 but it was not widely grown, perhaps because it is not a particularly showy plant. As a result, it was slow to escape and was not recorded in the wild for another 200 years but it didn't spread far, as individual plants simply sprang up and then vanished again. Beggarticks was what's called a 'casual' species, appearing in the wild briefly and then disappearing just as quickly, until unexpectedly in 1952 a patch of the plant was found on a canal towpath near Birmingham – at last it had become naturalized (see p.29). No one knows why it eventually took root, though perhaps it was in response to climate change or maybe an especially vigorous form of the plant took hold. What we do know is how far and wide it has since spread from Birmingham.

Like beggarticks, many plants have evolved so that their seeds are dispersed by animals – a mechanism known as zoochory. There are two ways in which animals can spread a plant's seeds: 1) by carrying them inside their bodies (endozoochory), usually by eating seed-bearing fruit and berries, which are passed through the animal's droppings and deposited in the soil with a handy dollop of fertilizer; 2) by carrying the seeds outside their bodies (epizoochory), whether stuck to their skin, hair, claws, whiskers or fur, as in the case of beggarticks. Each seed has

The trail of beggarticks along the Llangollen Canal in North Wales can be traced on the national distribution map for this towpath traveller (opposite).

two long spines at one end, shaped rather like a pitchfork; and the tip of each spine is barbed with tiny backward-facing teeth.

Once big patches of beggarticks had started growing alongside the canals of Birmingham, their seeds were picked up in the hairy coats of dogs that went nosing along the water's edge, often on the hunt for ducks and small mammals. As canal towpaths are very popular with walkers, who invariably like to exercise their dogs in different places each day, they very effectively spread the plant from one canal to another. Beggarticks has now been moved around the waterway network by thousands of owners and their dogs.

The map for beggarticks (inset top) today reveals Birmingham as the major hotspot for its spread, with other canals radiating outwards and looping around London (inset bottom). The increase of beggarticks along towpaths is aided by its barbed seeds.

BEGGARTICKS
BIDENS FRONDOSA

TODAY

DOG-PEE LICHENS

The base of many tree trunks in our cities harbour an eye-catching array of lichen species that you won't necessarily find outside urban areas. Taking a closer look, you might see bright splashes of lichen in lively yellows and stark greys, set against a velvety carpet of emerald algae. It's easy to get drawn into these little pockets of interest – but beware! To male dogs, this is the perfect place to shout, 'Spike woz 'ere', by adding their own personal 'marker' to the tree. That's right – these bright patches are fed by a constant supply of dog pee (right).

The nitrogen content of this marker is so high that few species can survive here, as the pollutant generally causes huge problems for wild things. For some species, though, such as *Prasiola crispa* and the

bright yellow *Candelariella reflexa*, the nitrogen pollutant in dog pee provides the perfect habitat where they often grow vigorously, having the place all to themselves.

Sally, Chris and Lottie examine the dog-pee zone of a tree in central Birmingham.

With over 160km of canals around Birmingham, it's no wonder that the city is now the major British hotspot for beggarticks, which shows up as a blur of dots on the distribution map for the plant (see p.117). Now, though, we can also make out other canals populated by beggarticks, radiating out from the central hub in Birmingham. Tracing the distinctive lines of dots on the plant's map, it's possible to follow the Trent Navigation heading northeast, the Llangollen Canal leading into North Wales and both the River Severn and the Avon Canal moving southwest. Further south, we can also pick out the southern end of the Grand Union Canal, the Regent's Canal and the River Lee Navigation, forming a loop around London.

Beggarticks is a plant still in the early stages of its spread, currently on a slow increase, finding its way to new places and quietly settling in among the native vegetation without causing any problems. Who knows, though, what the future will hold for beggarticks? It might stick to the canals, following their lines in the landscape, but more likely it will find its way to other suitable spots, such as rivers, lakes and ponds, and the beggarticks map of the future might not show the canal network as clearly as it does today.

AMERICAN PONDWEED

Although the name suggests otherwise, pondweeds can be found in rivers and canals, as well as in ponds. The mapping of one in particular, American pondweed (*Potamogeton epihydrus*), clearly shows its connection with canals.

Pondweeds are truly specialist aquatic plants that spend their entire lives underwater and have developed some remarkable biological tricks to survive: their pollen, for instance, can pass from flower to flower on the surface of the water, or rise in tiny air bubbles passed between male and female plants. Some pondweeds, however, such as red

The distinctive cluster of dots on the map for American pondweed (inset top) shows its occurrence in several canals between Leeds and Manchester, such as the Rochdale Canal (inset bottom). Its presence here is as mysterious as in the Outer Hebrides, where it is represented by two isolated dots (top left).

AMERICAN PONDWEED
POTAMOGETON EPIHYDRUS

TODAY

pondweed (*P. alpinus*) have suffered severe declines, badly affected by poor quality river water as well as by the infilling of village and farmland ponds. Other pondweeds have not only spread but done so mysteriously. American pondweed, for instance, is widespread in North America but, rather remarkably, in 1907 it turned up in the Calder and Hebble Navigation at Salterhebble Bridge in Halifax, northern England. Nobody knows how on earth this American plant found its way into a British canal. It's assumed to have been introduced at some point, but it can't have been easy to bring an aquatic species all the way from America and get it to grow in a muddy canal. Why would you, anyway? It's a pretty dull-looking thing with no ornamental value.

A Hebridean mystery

Today, American pondweed is also found in the Rochdale Canal in northern England, which can clearly be seen on the plant's distribution map (see p.119). Look again, though, and you'll spot two more dots, way off to the northwest in the remote Outer Hebrides of Scotland, where the weed was discovered in 1943. It still grows there in the pristine waters of a few shallow, peaty lochans (small lochs), miles from anywhere and certainly a very long way from the midland canals. These sites are so remote and untouched that American pondweed is considered to be native here, though how the plant made its way to Scotland in the distant past remains a mystery. Perhaps it's a relict of the time around 180 million years ago when the land masses of America and Europe lay closer together, before the Atlantic Ocean opened; or maybe its seeds took a transatlantic crossing on the feet, or in the stomachs, of migrating birds. We'll probably never know. Some things just defy explanation.

The pristine waters of a freshwater loch on South Harris in the Outer Hebrides, Scotland, are a long way from any muddy canals in the English midlands, but American pondweed grows in both.

GRACEFUL PONDWEED

Not only canals but also rivers can sometimes show up on the plant maps for pondweeds. Graceful pondweed (*Potamogeton x olivaceus*), the hybrid between red pondweed (*P. alpinus*) and curled pondweed (*P. crispus*), has spread along large lengths of both the River Teifi in southwest Wales and the River Tweed in the Scottish borders. Both rivers stand out clearly on the plant's distribution map, although not as wavy river lines but rather as two straight lines – a curious feature explained by the fact that rivers

GRACEFUL PONDWEED
POTAMOGETON X OLIVACEUS

TODAY

don't wander much on their downward flow to the sea. It's rare for individual rivers to stand out on the plant distribution maps so clearly, as aquatic plants often have excellent ways of getting around (see p.119) so tend to populate waterways across the country. Sometimes, though, the spread of less common non-native species that have escaped into just a few rivers can reveal such waterways very clearly, as in the case of graceful pondweed. What's puzzling about the hybrid is that neither of its parents (red and curled pondweeds) has ever been found in the River Teifi, suggesting that it is an ancient relict, a left-over from a time when the two parent pondweeds did grow and cross-breed in the river system.

Two clear lines on the distribution map for graceful pondweed (inset top) highlight the trail of the plant along the River Tweed in the Scottish borders and the River Teifi in southwest Wales (inset bottom).

NOOTKA LUPINS

No distribution map shows the courses of rivers more clearly than that for nootka lupin (*Lupinus nootkatensis*), a species that originated in western North America and northeast Asia. In their native home, nootka lupins grow on damp, gravelly soil, particularly the deep shingle banks that develop along rivers in upland areas. In the British Isles, too, the plant has gravitated to moist, northern latitudes and thrives in Scotland, where it was found for the first time growing in the wild in Aberdeenshire in 1862. The lupin had escaped from the grounds of Balmoral Castle, where it was planted during Queen Victoria's reign (1837–1901) and, feeling very much at home, had

The preference for a cool, northern climate is revealed in the map for nootka lupin (insets), which shows the course of several rivers in Scotland, including the Rivers Ness, Dee, Spey and Tay.

NOOTKA LUPIN
LUPINUS NOOTKATENSIS

TODAY

spread along the banks and shingle ridges of the River Dee. Since then it has colonized the length of three similar rivers – the Rivers Ness, Spey and Tay, all clearly visible on the map (see opposite).

As a plant of cold, damp climates, nootka lupin was particularly suitable for breeding the colourful cottage-garden Russell lupins (*Lupinus arboreus x polyphyllus*), so popular today because they can shrug off the worst of our summer weather. Russell lupins are now more common in gardens than the original nootka lupin, which is no longer widely grown. Its diminishing popularity, combined with our warmer climate, means that nootka lupins are now declining in Scotland but, for the time being at least, we can enjoy a little bit of North America in the Highlands.

Naturalized Russell lupins flourish beside the River Spey in Grantown-on-Spey, northern Scotland.

LOOKING TO THE FUTURE

Whether racing off to work, rushing around the shopping mall or taking the dog for a walk, we're all constantly on the move, making tracks across the landscape. Most trips are fringed by corridors of life where plants have found a variety of homes, ranging from roadside verges to railway embankments, from country lanes to canal towpaths. For many of us, glimpsing the local plant life on our daily rounds is the closest we'll ever get to connecting with the multitude of wild things that flourish in the linear habitats that we've created for them. It's worth making that connection, though, and plants will never fail to surprise us – as natural opportunists, they make the most of every chance to spread and take root in all manner of new homes.

Even when wildflower meadows or ancient woods are sometimes cleared to make way for roads and railways, scars can heal in time as a myriad wild things move in and flourish: bare railway embankments might be colonized by orchids; new pools can provide homes for frogs and newts; patches of regenerating scrub might serve as hunting grounds for birds of prey, until woodland develops once again.

As our need to travel increases and we create new linear habitats, many more opportunities for wild things will arise, and plants will continue to turn up in quite unexpected places. None of us could have predicted that a seaside species, such as Danish scurvygrass, would one day reach the hub of our transport network, but you never know what you're going to come across next.

CHAPTER FOUR
MOUNTAINS

PREVIOUS PAGE At 917m tall, the peak of Tryfan overlooks Llyn Ogwen in Snowdonia, North Wales, and is one of the most popular mountains to climb in the British Isles.

From the craggy slopes of Snowdonia in Wales to the highest peaks of the Cairngorms in Scotland, the British Isles are home to some stunning mountain ranges. Over 16 per cent of our land is more than 300m high, but with plunging winter temperatures, storm force winds, intense rainfall – 3m in the Scottish Highlands – and hardly any soil in which to gain a foothold, it's incredible how any form of plant manages to survive in such a habitat. It's not an easy life at the top, to say the least.

ABOVE Bilberry forms dense thickets on acidic soils. Its berries are a valuable food source for birds and other wildlife.

ABOVE RIGHT The flowers of bell heather turn the mountains purple in late summer and provide a feast for pollinating bees.

Yet look around any mountainous landscape in the British Isles and you'll see plants everywhere. From slopes clothed in bell heather (*Calluna vulgaris*) and bilberry (*Vaccinium myrtillus*) to deep mossy bogs; from dripping cliff faces to gurgling mountain streams lined with ferns, our mountains are home to some very special plants. Many arrived here more than 10,000 years ago, at the end of the last Ice Age, and are now ancient relicts of that time. In the past fifty years, however, we have seen a dramatic change taking place as some of these old survivors have started a steep decline.

Although at present just over 150 species of flowering plants and ferns can be found on the mountains of Britain and Ireland, nearly half of them are threatened. That's a higher proportion than in any other habitat in the British Isles – time to take stock …

JUNIPER

There's no doubt that a cold refreshing gin and tonic is one of our favourite tipples. Yet how many people actually realize that we might soon be running out of the main ingredient in the production of gin: juniper (*Juniperus communis*), for it's the juicy black juniper berry that gives gin its distinctively fresh, sharp taste.

Juniper has been with us for a very long time, since just after the last Ice Age, in fact. The retreating glaciers left a desolate landscape of bare rock and freshly ground-up sediments but these were soon colonized, first by mosses and lichens and later by small alpine plants, such as saxifrages (*Saxifraga*) and dwarf willow (*Salix herbacea*), which can still be seen on our mountains today (see pp.146–7).

Overlooking Llyn Llydaw in Snowdonia, North Wales, juniper clings precariously to the rock face.

ABOVE Juniper once dominated our mountain landscapes, but now often grows as isolated bushes, as seen here on the hills of Snowdonia in North Wales.

BELOW Juniper berries provide a valuable food source for birds and small mammals.

These early plants were true pioneer species, which moved into the bare, open frontier ground, formed by the retreating glaciers, before anything else could gain a foothold. Juniper was one of the first substantial woody plants to colonize the newly vegetated landscape. It formed dense thickets on lower slopes, while higher up the mountain, the juniper scrub grew more open and many other plants, such as royal fern (*Osmunda regalis*) and meadow-rue (*Thalictrum*), grew alongside it in a rich mix of vegetation. For a time, though, juniper dominated. Through a remarkable mechanism that allows it to survive severe cold, it spread through the British Isles (see pp.132–3).

A bush in crisis

Despite juniper's ability to survive extreme conditions, we've noticed a dramatic change in the plant's well-being over the past fifty years. It is now much rarer in the British Isles than it was half a century ago. We now have to face up to the fact that this plant is in crisis; in some parts of Britain, it is disappearing. Yet, if we compare the most recent distribution map for juniper with that created in 1962, there doesn't seem to be much change. The dots have only disappeared

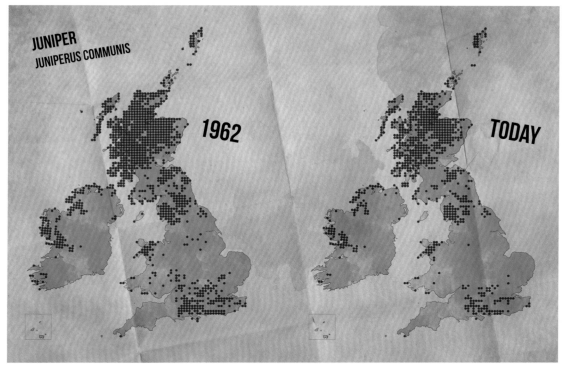

JUNIPER
JUNIPERUS COMMUNIS

1962

TODAY

from a few areas, such as southern England. You'd be forgiven for thinking that nothing's really wrong. In northern Wales, northern England and especially in Scotland, the map is solid with dots. So what's the worry? To find out, we should look beyond the national picture and dig a bit deeper.

A closer look at the 10km squares

The distribution maps are based on the Ordnance Survey system of dividing the whole of Britain and Ireland into a regular grid of 10km squares or 'hectads' (see pp.25–6). If a particular plant is found in a particular hectad, then it gets a dot on the map, no matter how many plants are actually present, whether one or 1,000. To see how many juniper bushes exist at ground level, we need to scrutinize one of the hectads (see overleaf). If we look closely, we can see a sprinkling of coloured dots, which tell a story: the spattering of thirteen red dots shows where a single bush has survived; the seventeen black dots mark dead bushes that have disappeared; and the nine green dots indicate where several bushes are growing together. But there aren't many green dots, and that's what matters.

Comparison of the two maps for juniper doesn't show a huge difference over the last fifty years. Large tracts, especially in the uplands of the north and west of the British Isles, still remain quite thickly covered with dots. It's only when we look more closely at the ground that the true story emerges (see p.130).

JUNIPER AT GROUND LEVEL

To see how well juniper is doing, look at the coloured dots on the map (right), which reveal the state of all juniper bushes found within a single 10km square in the mountains of Snowdonia, North Wales.

KEY
- A single live bush
- A single dead bush
- Several live bushes

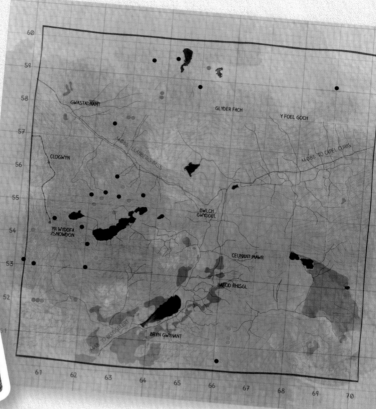

- **A single live bush** (*top*) Across large areas of Snowdonia, all that remain are solitary, isolated bushes, which are effectively doomed, as juniper bushes are either male or female, so a single bush cannot produce berries and seed for a new generation (see pp.141–2).

- **A single dead bush** (*middle*) Sad-looking remnants of old juniper bushes dotted around the landscape remind us of how these mountains would once have been covered in this incredible plant.

- **Several live bushes growing together** (*bottom*) In a few areas, there's a glimmer of hope, perhaps? There are small pockets with between five and ten bushes and even one or two places where you can find between fifty and 100 small bushes growing together.

FROM JUNIPER TO GIN

- Gin actually gets its name from the Dutch *jenever* or the Old French *genièvre*, based in turn on the Latin *juniperus*, meaning juniper.

- Juniper berries provide the bitter, resin-like quality unique to the spirit. This flavour comes from the pinene molecule – a strong-smelling monoterpene (volatile organic compound) that also gives pine tree resin its distinctive scent (see p.69). A host of other botanical flavourings all lend their own qualities to the final tipple, including almond, angelica, liquorice, lemon, cardamom and coriander.

- It was the Dutch who invented gin as we know it today – a grain spirit re-distilled with various flavourings. Large-scale production of gin was underway in Holland by the seventeenth century and its calming effect on Dutch troops during the Thirty Years' War (1618–48) led to the phrase 'Dutch courage'.

Chris, Sally and Trevor (above) enjoy an al fresco gin in the mountains. The berries that give gin its taste (below) take three years to ripen, with fresh green berries growing alongside ripe black ones on the same bush.

- Gin production in England increased around the same time, after the government allowed its unlicensed production, leading to the spirit's reputation in the eighteenth century as 'Mother's ruin', a social problem graphically portrayed in William Hogarth's satire of drunkards in *Gin Lane* (1751).

- In the nineteenth century, juniper was abundant enough in the Scottish Highlands for its berries to be collected by locals and for a whole industry to be born. Bagfuls were taken to the Inverness and Aberdeen markets from where they were exported to the Dutch gin distillers.

- Unfortunately, the Scottish industry has since disappeared. Today, most of the juniper berries now used to flavour the gin produced in the British Isles come from Europe, especially Italy and countries of the former Yugoslavia. Some experts say that juniper berries grown in warm climates produce sweeter-tasting oils, which provide the key ingredients in the taste of gin.

What makes juniper a survivor?

Unlike many other plants, this hardy little conifer can survive the coldest and harshest of winters, just as it endured the arctic conditions that gripped the British Isles for thousands of years after the last Ice Age, around 10,000 years ago.

The equipment
1 x 12m refrigerated lorry
1 x thermal imaging camera
2 x very warm hats
1 x sprig of juniper
1 x sprig of dogwood

It's not every day that you have reason to hire a 12m refrigerated, articulated lorry, our 'arctic artic', but the *Wild Things* team wanted to discover just how juniper survives icy temperatures – what clever tricks it might have evolved to endure the arctic climate

Even in the snow, juniper is a happy little conifer and shrugs off the cold (above), while in their refrigerated lorry laboratory (below), Trevor and Chris put a juniper and dogwood leaf to the test.

after the Ice Age. With the help of our arctic artic and with a thermal imaging camera, this experiment reveals how juniper survives the freezing cold.

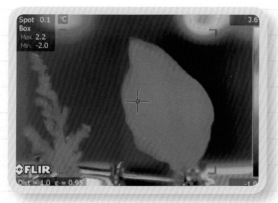

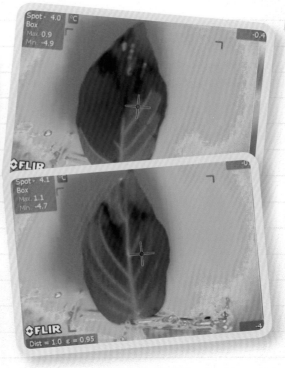

The method

Under a thermal imaging camera, warmer objects show up as red and yellow, and colder ones as blue and black. A sprig of juniper and a leaf of dogwood were set up for comparison. The temperature was then dropped to minus 6°C. As it got colder, the camera showed the two plants changing colour from red to yellow and then to dark blue at the freezing point of 0°C.

As the temperature plummeted, you might have expected the water inside both leaves to freeze and turn to ice. In fact, when the water dropped slightly below freezing, at first no ice formed, although the water became super-cooled. The picture then changed quite dramatically. In the dogwood leaf, a crystal of ice suddenly materialized, which triggered the surrounding water to produce more ice, in turn creating a wave of sharp ice crystals that ripped destructively through the leaf in just a few seconds.

THE SCIENCE

Remarkably and rather counter-intuitively, when an ice crystal forms it gives off a tiny amount of heat because the final 'bit' of heat in a freezing liquid must be lost, or the freezing process itself will grind to a halt. And here our thermal camera came into play – it showed that final tiny burst of heat as pale blue, allowing us to watch the ice forming within the leaf. The sharp ice crystals very quickly destroyed the dogwood leaf, with effects similar to an overnight hard frost on garden plants.

Thermal images of the juniper and dogwood leaves (above left) eventually changed colour to dark blue as the temperature fell. Just below 0°C, pale blue ice crystals started to rip through the dogwood leaf (top), destroying all its cells (above). By contrast, juniper remained unchanged, as the anti-freeze prevented ice from causing any damage.

By comparison, no sharp ice crystals formed within the juniper sprig. It simply soaked up the arctic conditions, essentially because juniper has evolved a remarkable tactic for surviving the cold: its own special anti-freeze that operates deep within its cells. When the temperature drops, the plant releases thousands of anti-freeze proteins, which smother the spiky ice crystals that would ordinarily puncture and destroy the cell walls and delicate membranes of a plant's leaves. With its natural anti-freeze, juniper can react fast before any damage occurs. The plant is clearly a survivor. Not only does it shrug off the potential damage caused by ice crystals, but it also carries on with its daily life, functioning well below 0°C.

Unlike so many other plants, juniper survives winter, alive and undamaged. Its unique anti-freeze capability enabled the plant to thrive in the arctic conditions at the end of the Ice Age.

Home to an entire ecosystem

Juniper supports an amazing variety of wild things that shelter within its branches and feed on its leaves, berries, stems or roots. Seventy-five species of insect have been associated with juniper in the British Isles. They include mites, aphids, scale insects, leaf webbers, leaf miners, micro-moths and gall wasps. Of these, forty-three feed exclusively on juniper, such as the juniper shield bug. With its specially adapted mouthparts, much like a retractable hypodermic needle, this insect stabs the plant's tough leaves and extracts the thick resin. All these insects in turn provide a valuable food source for a whole range of birds, such as crested tits, found only in Scotland's Caledonian Forest (see pp.74–5). The berries themselves feed upland birds, such as the mistle thrush, ring ouzel and fieldfares. The

A community of wild things associated with juniper, from left to right: the juniper shield bug, a camouflaged moth caterpillar, ring ouzel and juniper rust fungus.

bushes also provide valuable shelter for black grouse and other small birds and mammals.

Many fungi and slime-moulds – up to 496 species – are also directly associated with juniper. Two remarkable rust fungi (*Gymnosporangium clavariiforme* and *G. cornutum*) spend half their life cycle on juniper, where they form branching, coral-like growths. These produce spores that drift in the wind and land on rowan trees (*Sorbus aucuparia*) or hawthorn bushes (*Crataegus monogyna*), where they either form yellowish lesions on the leaves, or infect the fruit, creating tiny tubes. These lesions and tubes produce other spores that blow back to the juniper plant, completing the complex life cycle of this colourful fungus.

Losing more than a berry

If juniper disappears from our landscape, these largely unseen mini-ecosystems will fade away too. We stand to lose a whole community of wild things, not just juniper itself – and that is alarming. After all this time, since just after the last Ice Age, it's incredible to think that this multifaceted plant now might be near its end. We can't let it disappear 'on our watch'.

In the Cairngorm Mountains, Scotland, Trevor searches for
some of the unique wild things that live only on juniper.

FLOWERING TIMES

	J	F	M	A	M	J	J	A	S	O	N	D
Juniper	✿	✿	✿	✿	✿	✿	✿	✿	✿	✿	✿	✿

Where have all the seedlings gone?

Even where juniper bushes appear to be growing together in clusters, as on the hills of Snowdonia (see p.130), if we look more closely at the ground, we'll see that something is not quite right. There are no youngsters around, no vigorous new seedlings that will grow up and replace the mature bushes once they die.

Unfortunately the story is the same in most other parts of the British Isles, even in Scotland where the distribution map for juniper seems solid with dots (see p.129). True, if you head off to the Highlands of Scotland, especially to the Cairngorms National Park with its old Caledonian pinewoods (*Pinus sylvestris*), you'll see juniper at its finest – an abundance of juniper, scattered throughout the landscape. Within Scotland's pinewoods, the plant forms a

THE TALL AND THE SHORT OF IT

Juniper bushes vary enormously in their appearance. Some are tall and some are short. Some stand upright like trees and others lie flat to the ground, hugging every contour of the rock. They look so different that they're often given different names: common juniper (*J. communis* subsp. *communis*) for the tall tree and prostrate juniper (*J. communis* subsp. *nana*) for the short one. But the latest genetic research shows that the two types are actually one and the same.

Walk into any pub and line everyone up along the bar, with the shortest at one end and the tallest at the other, and there'll be a complete range of heights in between. Tall or short, they're still all people, just people of different heights. It's the same with juniper and in some populations in the mountains you

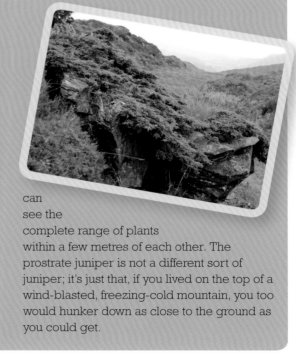

can see the complete range of plants within a few metres of each other. The prostrate juniper is not a different sort of juniper; it's just that, if you lived on the top of a wind-blasted, freezing-cold mountain, you too would hunker down as close to the ground as you could get.

dense layer of bushes, known as an 'understorey', which grows under the forest's canopy of tall trees. On still, warm days, the juniper bushes add to that fresh resin smell that hangs in the air. Elsewhere in the Highlands, entire open hillsides are clothed with the plant, which forms its own dwarf forests. Wonderful gnarled bushes grow with big twisting branches. Mature juniper bushes predominate in the full glory of their life, with the female bushes laden with dark, ripe berries. Once again, though, there are precious few seedlings around.

One of the main problems is that juniper takes a very long time, up to fifteen years, to grow and reach maturity, before producing the berries that create the next generation. Once grown, though, the plant lives for a long time. Remarkably, juniper bushes can survive for over 250 years, but now these 'old grandfathers' are slowly ageing and dying naturally. What we need are new seedlings coming through to create the next generation of bushes. Unfortunately, this simply isn't happening any more, which is why juniper's future is uncertain and why it is regarded as one of the most important plants to watch. Crucially, we need to discover exactly why its seedlings seem to be so thin on the ground.

A thicket of juniper growing under birch in the Cairngorms National Park, Scotland.

Why is juniper struggling?

Reviewing the latest evidence provided by the distribution maps for juniper, it's now clear that the plant has declined dramatically in mountain ranges, such as Snowdonia in North Wales. Even in Scotland, where the plant flourishes in some areas, it's been lost from a quarter of the places where it once grew (see p.129). Three separate factors have combined to create difficulties for juniper: 1) sheep-grazing; 2) mountain fires; and 3) slow and patchy reproduction.

 ### Sheep *versus* cattle

From the sixteenth to the early nineteenth century, cattle were widely grazed in the Welsh mountains. Breeds such as the Welsh Black were moved to upland pastures (called the 'Hafod') during the summer and then returned to the shelter of lowland pastures (the 'Hendre') during the winter. This style of seasonal farming was good for plants such as juniper. The pattern of grazing by heavy animals achieved two things: it opened up the ground (big cows produce big hoof marks); and it gave the mountain pastures a seasonal break. Both features were ideal for juniper, because seeds could germinate in the open, disturbed ground; and with half the year relatively free of cattle, seedlings had a better chance of reaching adulthood without being nibbled.

LOWLAND JUNIPER

Juniper is not just a mountain plant but is also found in the lowlands. In the mountains it tends to grow on acidic rocks, but in the lowlands it thrives on rocks rich in lime. The plant therefore commonly grows on limestone, especially in the English Cotswolds and on the Welsh Gower Peninsula and Great Orme. As lowland juniper also survives on chalk, it's found on Salisbury Plain, on the North and South Downs and the Chilterns in England. Unfortunately, the lowlands, much like the uplands, have experienced a decline in the number of juniper bushes over the past fifty years.

Towards the end of the seventeenth century, however, the wool industry began to dominate, which led to an increase in sheep-grazing over the next two centuries. Sheep-grazing increased again during the twentieth century throughout the 1980s and 1990s when farmers were encouraged by European Union policy and payments to stock more sheep. Today, there are twenty-five times more sheep in some areas than there were in medieval times.

Unfortunately, although sheep have sustained the farming industry and allowed families to make a living in the uplands, they've had a damaging effect on the plants of northern England and Snowdonia. Sheep nibble and graze everywhere all the time, rather like thousands of hairdressers' scissors, snipping and trimming away. Unlike cattle, they remain up in the hills all year round and, as a result, not only nibble plant seedlings but also trim everything back very neatly and evenly. In their wake, a thick dense sward (mat of short grass) develops, which is not good news for plants and other wild things. The dense grass mat prevents seeds from gaining a foothold and smothers any seedlings that do emerge. It's not just sheep that are out there nibbling the seedlings, though. In Scotland and northern England deer are doing it, too, and their numbers in Scotland are thought to have doubled in the last fifty years. Although

Chris helps to herd a flock of sheep off the mountains in Snowdonia, North Wales. Maintaining the right level of grazing with beneficial livestock is essential if mountain plants, such as juniper, are to thrive.

deer are larger and heavier animals than sheep, their year-round grazing leads to the development of the same thick, grassy swards on the mountains. As juniper seeds consistently fail to germinate in the dense sward and as sheep and deer continue to nibble any seedlings, much of our mountain juniper has now retreated to the steepest crags and most inaccessible cliffs beyond the reach of grazing animals.

A burning issue

Another enemy of the juniper plant is fire. For some mountain plants, controlled fire can be beneficial. Mountain heathland, for instance, is regularly burnt in order to keep heather young and growing well. Controlled burning is a quick and easy way of managing overgrown heather because, when heather is set alight, the old, woody plants burn quickly, but they're not killed. New shoots grow readily from the base of the plant, relishing the nutrients released from the ash. Put fire and juniper together, though, and you don't get a 'happy ever after'. Unlike heather,

Controlled burning is a common way of rejuvenating overgrown heather, which later reshoots from the base. But such fires are deadly to juniper, which perishes in the flames.

juniper cannot regenerate from new shoots and is extremely sensitive to fire. Like most other conifers, the plant produces an abundance of resin, a thick fluid full of turpenes (special hydrocarbons that help protect the plant from attack by fungal infections, insects and grazing animals). As these chemicals are volatile and extremely flammable, juniper catches fire easily and goes up like an inferno, burning quickly at a very high temperature. If the fire is very hot, which it usually is when burning heather, the juniper plants are killed completely. Whole populations have been wiped out by single fires. Once gone, they never seem to return to the burnt hillside.

 Lone survivors

Quite apart from having to endure attack by nibbling sheep and heathland fires, junipers don't make life easy for themselves either. Unlike most plants, which have both male and female parts within their flowers, junipers don't, as they are 'dioecious', which means that each bush is either male or female.

THE HANGING GARDENS OF SNOWDONIA

In Snowdonia in North Wales, many rare and special mountain plants can still be found on near vertical cliffs and crags – well away from nibbling animals. Facing north, these are often cool and damp and drip constantly with water from the mountains above. Here in the shade, a thick, luxuriant growth can develop, reminiscent of a woodland floor and appearing very out of place in the starkly grazed hills around them. The best examples of hanging gardens are perhaps in Cwm Idwal (right), a basin (cwm) backing the glacial lake Llyn Idwal. Cwm Idwal's hanging gardens flank either side of the narrow defile known as the Devil's Kitchen. Some particularly lush and colourful varieties of plant life include the exotic-looking early-purple orchid (*Orchis mascula*), the aptly named globeflower (*Trollius europaeus*), umbrella-like wild angelica (*Angelica sylvestris*), the evergreen wood-rush (*Luzula sylvatica*) and pretty wood anemone (*Anemone nemorosa*).

The male plant produces only pollen while the female, once pollinated, produces only berries, which contain the seed for the next generation. With a large group of bushes, single-sex plants don't pose any problem: male and female junipers growing together can produce berries. When you're down to just a few isolated bushes, though, dioecy becomes a real problem. Unless both male and female bushes grow closely together, the seed-bearing berries are unlikely to be produced; and if you're the last surviving bush in an area, as is so often the case now, you're going to be living a rather monk-like, celibate lifestyle, with not much hope of any offspring.

Even when bushes have mated, the production of seeds in juniper is painfully slow. In the majority of plants, pollination takes place and seeds are set a few weeks later, which then go on to germinate within a year. Not so with juniper: amazingly, it can take up to six years after pollination before the seeds germinate. Juniper seeds also need a certain number of 'frost-days', when they're frozen, before they will grow. In fact germination is faster in the Arctic where frost-days can be clocked up more quickly.

TOP *Seeds extracted from juniper berries. Each berry usually contains between one and three seeds.*

ABOVE *A bountiful harvest of ripe juniper berries, containing seed for the next generation.*

JUNIPER SEED CALENDAR

Here's the normal course of events for the production of juniper seeds:

Year 1: Pollination takes place in the spring, but the pollen is stored away by the flower.

Year 2: The stored pollen grains finally fertilize the flowers and the green berry begins to swell.

Year 3: The berries ripen, turning black, drop from the bush or get eaten by birds and eventually find their way to the soil – the seeds are 'planted'.

Year 4: The cold of the first winter tells the seed that it's had one winter. It remains dormant.

Year 5: The cold of the second winter tells the seed that it's had two winters. It remains dormant.

Year 6: The cold of the third winter tells the seed that it's had three winters. It finally germinates.

THREE BRITISH CONIFERS

The British Isles are home to only three native conifers: juniper (*J. communis*), Scots pine (*Pinus sylvestris*) and yew (*Taxus baccata*). The rest of the conifers growing here were originally brought from abroad.

Needle-thin leaves

The leaves of Scots pine and juniper are thin and needle-like, reducing water-loss, but those of yew are slightly flattened (below).

On home ground

Scots pine (above) is native to Scotland, where remnants of the once great Caledonian Forest offer a glimpse of what much of Britain once looked like shortly after the Ice Age. Scots pine has been widely planted throughout the British Isles, where it often regenerates on acidic soils. Yew is thought to be native to southern England, the Welsh borders and upland areas of northern England. By now, it has been widely planted in the wild throughout the British Isles, often in churchyards. Juniper is now found mostly in Scotland and northern England, but also in North Wales and central southern England (see p.129).

Juniper berries (below) are used to flavour game, bread and cakes, as well as beer and gin, while yew berries (left) should be avoided, as their seed is highly toxic. Scots pine (top) produces scaly, inedible cones.

Spreading seed

Most conifers, such as Scots pine, produce scaly cones, which contain seed, but both yew (above) and juniper (right) yield seed-bearing berries instead. The fleshy berries are attractive to birds, which eat the fruity part and swallow the seeds, depositing them in their droppings. In this way, seed can be spread far from its parent tree. Unlike juniper berries, those of yew have no culinary use, as most parts of the plant, including the seed, are extremely toxic. Although the red fleshy part of the berry is not actually poisonous, it's best avoided.

A glimmer at the end of the pass

Although some experts have predicted that in the next fifty years we could face a British landscape with hardly any juniper growing at all, certain signs offer a glimmer of hope. Establishing the right conditions for the plant to recover in the uplands is not difficult, and efforts to do so are already starting to pay off. It all depends on creative grazing, land management and some judicious planting.

At several sites where sizeable populations of both male and female plants survive, reduced sheep-grazing has allowed seedlings to grow. There's still, however, the thick sward of grass to contend with (see p.139). In an effort to break it up, cattle have been reintroduced since the 1990s, with Welsh blacks returning to the Welsh uplands and Highland cattle to Scottish pastures. Seedlings, hundreds in some cases, have started to appear in upland and lowland areas. Such land management techniques are creating better conditions, allowing this hardy plant to grow.

The lonely survivors still need our help – individual bushes could benefit from a bit of encouragement on the dating front. In an effort to bolster some of these populations, juniper plants of different sexes are often cultivated and planted out into the wild, bringing male and female bushes together again.

Magnificent Highland cattle provide the right combination of seasonal grazing and disturbed soil that juniper seedlings need to survive.

A future for juniper?

Because juniper is now in such dire straits, various government and conservation organizations, such as Plantlife, have spent much time and effort in monitoring the situation and trying to work out how best to reverse the plant's decline. As juniper has flourished in the British Isles for more than 10,000 years, it seems only proper that this 'old grandfather' should be allowed to survive for generations to come. It would, indeed, be a sad state of affairs if we were to allow one of our most treasured and iconic plants to die out during our lifetime.

Hopefully, our concerted efforts, combined with continued adjustments to land management and farming practices, will see a positive upturn in the fate of the plant. You never know, with some goodwill and effort, there could even be a 'happy ever after' story for juniper after all. Let's raise a glass of gin and tonic and drink to the good health of juniper.

The lakes of Llynnau Mymbyr look towards the high peaks of Snowdonia, North Wales, where juniper once flourished.

ARCTIC-ALPINES

On some stretches of mountainside, where the soil is thin and acidic, tracts of moor and heath can roll on for miles with the same few plants, such as acid-loving heathers and grasses. But where there is some lime in the rock, as at Cwm Idwal in Snowdonia, the uplands can be crammed with rarities (see opposite).

Many of our rarer mountain plants are known as arctic-alpines because they are found in other cold parts of the world, such as the Arctic and the European Alps. In the British Isles they're regarded as relict populations, all that's left of once bigger communities that developed at the end of the last Ice Age. For a time, many dominated the landscape, exploiting the bare rock and abundant minerals exposed after the retreat of the ice sheets. As the climate warmed, new plants arrived: juniper, pine and birch, then oak and ash. Gradually the alpine plants that had once held sway across the country retreated up the mountains where thin soils and cold prevented forests from growing. On the summits, arctic-alpines, such as dwarf willow (*Salix herbacea*), still cling on today. In our milder, wetter climate, they're now restricted to the highest and coldest mountainsides – the arctic-alpine paradises (see opposite).

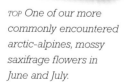

TOP One of our more commonly encountered arctic-alpines, mossy saxifrage flowers in June and July.

ABOVE Alpine penny-cress (Noccaea caerulescens) is restricted to mountains where the soil is enriched with lead or zinc (see p.44).

OUR ALPINE TREASURES

Saxifrages are well-known alpine plants, often grown in gardens on rockeries and borders, but we have many native mountain saxifrages too, some of which are extremely rare.

Common species	Where found
Mossy saxifrage (*Saxifraga hypnoides*)	England, Wales and Scotland
Purple saxifrage (*S. oppositifolia*)	England, Wales and Scotland
Starry saxifrage (*S. stellaris*)	England, Wales and Scotland
Yellow saxifrage (*S. aizoides*)	Lake District and Scotland
Rare species	**Where found**
Alpine saxifrage (*S. nivalis*)	England, Wales and Scotland
Drooping saxifrage (*S. cernua*)	Scotland
Highland saxifrage (*S. rivularis*)	Scotland
Tufted saxifrage (*S. cespitosa*)	Wales and Scotland

Arctic-alpine paradises

Our highest mountains are home to many rare plants, which flourish on the cold north-facing cliffs, especially where snow lies late in the year in sheltered snow-beds. Here are three of the best.

Ben Lawers, Perth and Kinross

The tenth highest peak in the Scottish Highlands, Ben Lawers (1,214m) is a botanical paradise and the number-one mountain for rare alpine plants in the British Isles (right). Of almost mythical status, its slopes are home to plants whose names conjure up their lush mountain paradise: alpine forget-me-not (*Myosotis alpestris*), Highland saxifrage (*S. rivularis*), woolly willow (*Salix lanata*), mountain saffron lichen (*Solorina crocea*) and rusty alpine psora (*Psora rubiformis*).

Helvellyn and Nethermost Pike, the Lake District, Cumbria

The northern slopes of the Helvellyn (950m) and Nethermost Pike (891m) peaks in the Helvellyn Range in Cumbria are home to some of the richest arctic-alpine and hanging garden habitats in England (below). Rare plants, such as downy willow (*Salix lapponum*) and alpine lady's mantle (*Alchemilla alpina*) are found no further south in Britain. Other specialities include alpine cinquefoil (*Potentilla crantzii*) and alpine mouse-ear (*Cerastium alpinum*).

Cwm Idwal, Snowdonia

A luxuriant hanging valley on the slopes of the Glyderau Mountains in Snowdonia (1,001m), Cwm Idwal is probably the most accessible site for rare alpine plants (below). Reached by a short circular walk around its breathtaking valley lake, Llyn Idwal, Cwm Idwal is home to the fabled Snowdon lily (*Lloydia serotina*), found only on the slopes of Snowdonia. The hanging gardens are crammed with other rarities, such as Welsh poppies (*Meconopsis cambrica*), saxifrages and scarce ferns, including tufted saxifrage (*S. cespitosa*) and holly fern (*Polystichum lonchitis*).

To the north of Loch Tay, Ben Lawers (above) is a mecca for climbers and naturalists, while Helvellyn in the Lake District (left) has long attracted botanists and poets, such as William Wordsworth; and Cwm Idwal in Snowdonia (below), with its remarkable outcrop of lime-rich volcanic rocks, drew naturalist Charles Darwin in the nineteenth century.

SUMMIT LICHENS

Pummelling winds, icy temperatures and sporadic rainfall that can bring flood, drought, hail and snow, all in a single day, mean that wild things making their home on our mountains have to be highly adapted to extreme conditions to survive. As altitude increases, survival becomes more and more gruelling with the harsh climate and thin to non-existent soils thwarting many flowering plants. At very high altitudes we find a place that is ruled by lichens and mosses.

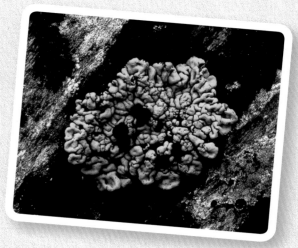

The rare goblin lights is found on the cold heights of Ben Nevis (1344m), gleaming in dark crevices.

Hardiness in the harshest of conditions

Although only 2.5 per cent of the British Isles lies above 610m altitude, at least 8 per cent of our bryophytes (mosses and liverworts) live here with over 15 per cent

The snow-covered mountainside of Y Lliwedd (898m) in North Wales is a harsh place for most plants to survive.

of our lichens. It is one of our most natural, untouched habitats and, as a result, is home to many a rare species. One of the most distinctive is goblin lights (*Catolechia wahlenbergii*), a Nationally Rare lichen that forms bright yellow patches, lighting up otherwise dark crevices in the rock.

Unfortunately some lichen species that live on our tallest mountains haven't been

seen for over twenty years. It's thought that these lost plants may be casualties of climate change: already occupying the highest altitudes, there is nowhere for these cold-adapted species to move to as the climate warms. In an effort to find the right conditions for their survival, they can quite literally fall off the tops of mountains. There is concern that more and more species will be lost in this way, if temperatures continue to rise.

The aptly named reindeer moss sustains reindeer during the harsh winter months.

Sheltered snow-beds

Compared to mountain tops, snow-beds are an altogether more sheltered place to live. These are magical habitats found on the flanks of mountains, where pockets of snow lie from early autumn well on into the summer. The largest patches are found year round, only melting around once in every twenty-five years. Though the word 'snow' does not conjure the image of a snug place to settle, many lichens, bryophytes and ferns do find these snowy spots bed-like, protected from the worst of the alpine weather by a 'cosy' blanket of icy snow. Believe it or not, snow acts as an insulator, protecting anything growing below from the icy weather above, just like a duvet. Ferns, such as alpine lady fern (*Athyrium distentifolium*), mosses and liverworts, such as the snow threadwort (*Pleurocladula albescens*), and lichens, such as the lovely *Lecanora leptacina*, all grow in these habitats. Such species are relicts from the end of the last Ice Age, *c*.10,000 years ago, when snow-beds would have covered vast areas of Britain. Today such plants grow in these snowiest of areas and nowhere else.

Reindeer pasture

The Cairngorms in Scotland comprise the largest area of high ground in the British Isles and have one of the harshest climates to match. During the winter these mountains are a dangerous place to be; however, a herd of reintroduced reindeer, an animal once native to Britain and commonly associated with arctic conditions, has been surviving in these mountains for over seventy years. During the winter, when the climate is at its fiercest, the reindeer turn to a most unlikely food source to stave off hunger. They manage to survive eating nothing much but the aptly named reindeer moss (*Cladonia rangifera*). This insignificant-looking miniature 'shrub' is in fact a lichen that carpets the ground in mountainous places. An unlikely source of sustenance for one of our largest mammals!

WELSH POPPY

Although many of our mountain plants seem to have become rarer over the past fifty years, certain species that were once found only in our uplands have now created a new home for themselves throughout the British Isles – right outside our own front doors, in fact.

The delicate and exotic-looking Welsh poppy (*Meconopsis cambrica*) is one of the top ten native plants that are on the increase in Britain and Ireland. How can this be? Our native Welsh poppy loves wet, rocky and shaded places. It grows in woodland, alongside rivers and up into the mountains, where it's found on damp, shaded cliffs, often beside streams. So what's a plant of moist, shady uplands and woodlands doing in almost every part of the British Isles?

We have to trace the story back to the plant's early history. The first mention of the Welsh poppy growing in the wild in the British Isles dates back to a record from Snowdonia of 1609. It soon became known as a plant of the Welsh uplands, which is probably how the poppy picked up its 'Welsh' tag.

WELSH POPPY
MECONOPSIS CAMBRICA

1962   TODAY

These magnificent flowers immediately grabbed the attention of gardeners, and we know that by 1732 Welsh poppies were growing in an English garden in Kent. The poppy proved to be a popular choice for gardens; and, before long, escapes into the wild were recorded in various parts of Britain, such as Kendal in Cumbria in 1778, but these early escapes didn't spread far.

Things remained much the same for many years until the twentieth century, when the plant suddenly started to spread. As the national maps show, the increase even in the last fifty years has been spectacular (see opposite). Welsh poppies are now widespread, growing on roadsides, walls, banks and waste ground, jumping over the garden wall at every opportunity and spreading even to the most remote spots, such as the Isle of Man and the Shetland Islands. What could have caused the change?

A Pyrenean heritage

Recent work on the genetics of this plant has shown that the Welsh poppy that has been growing in our gardens since the eighteenth century is not actually Welsh at all. It comes instead from seed of

BELOW LEFT In its natural upland habitat, native Welsh poppies thrive in damp, rocky enclaves, especially beside streams and waterfalls, such as the lush, water-drenched ledges of Cwm Idwal in Snowdonia, North Wales.

BELOW A firm favourite for gardens, our Welsh poppy has now escaped and spread to many parts of the British Isles, and today grows in very different habitats from its mountain home.

Native Welsh poppies are only ever pure yellow. Variable colours, such as the orange ones here on a roadside in North Wales, are sure signs of a non-native heritage. They originally came from the Pyrenees in France and are more genetically variable than our native poppies, making them more tolerant and better able to spread.

Welsh poppy collected in Europe – the central and eastern Pyrenees to be precise. It seems that, at some point in their history, poppies from this part of Europe were introduced into British gardens. Although they appear exactly the same as our native poppies growing in the wild and often found on our mountains, they are in fact genetically different. It is the variance in their DNA that seems to have helped them to spread.

Exactly why the Pyrenean poppy should be 'better' at spreading than our own native variety is not clear. At some point, gardeners must have inadvertently selected this variety, perhaps because it grew stronger and produced more flowers and seed, or maybe its seed germinated more easily than the other varieties. The Pyreneans are certainly more variable, with flowers available in orange and red as well as in doubles, so perhaps they are more genetically diverse and better able to cope with a wider range of conditions. As a result, the Pyreneans were distributed widely through garden centres and seed suppliers. Without realizing it, people would have grown increasing numbers of the Pyrenean poppies in their gardens from where they could quite easily escape into the wild.

Clearly, Pyrenean poppies are here to stay and they're certainly on the increase, but their expansion across the country doesn't seem to be causing too much harm – in fact they definitely add a splash of bright colour to the side of our roads. Unfortunately, though, just as the Pyrenean is becoming more widespread, our pure native populations seem to be dwindling, possibly as a result of both climate change and increased sheep-grazing on our hills and mountains (see pp.138–9).

Pure populations?

Since the Pyrenean is now out and about in the wild, we might wonder whether it's likely to cross with our Welsh poppy? At the moment, the mountain populations remain pure and there's no evidence that non-native genes have entered the Welsh gene pool. In the lowlands, however, some exchange of genes has already taken place, in much the same way that our native bluebells have crossed with the Spanish newcomers (see pp.58–61). Eventually, it may be that the gene pools of the Pyrenean and Welsh poppies will completely merge but, since both poppies tend to look the same, this might not be a problem. In fact, if our native plants are declining, perhaps they need a bit of a genetic boost to keep them going.

NEW ZEALAND WILLOWHERB

Just like many other habitats throughout the British Isles, our mountains serve as sensitive barometers of climate change. For plants that prefer the colder conditions higher up, climate change could have a profound effect on their survival. If they retreat further up our mountains, it will be yet another indication of how climate change is affecting our landscape. If global warming continues, eventually our mountain plants could run out of uplands to climb.

Other signs of climate change are the arrival and spread of new plants. Some, such as the tiny New Zealand willowherb (*Epilobium brunnescens*), can creep in unnoticed and populate even our remotest mountains. The rise in temperature, too, might affect a plant's behaviour – given the right sort of conditions, even the quiet ones have the potential to turn into pests.

The diminutive New Zealand willowherb, just less than a centimetre tall, has managed to creep into every part of western and northern Britain since its arrival in Scotland a century ago. Exactly why this New Zealand creeper was cultivated in British

After arriving in Scotland in 1904, the tiny New Zealand willowherb (inset) spread rapidly across the British Isles. By 1962, it had appeared in much of northern and western Britain, where it has now become common.

NEW ZEALAND WILLOWHERB
EPILOBIUM BRUNNESCENS

1962

TODAY

gardens is not entirely clear. True, gardeners do have an insatiable desire to cultivate as many different plants as possible but the New Zealand creeper has no obvious real ornamental value, despite its neatly arranged leaves and unusual brown tinge. Possibly, it made its way here in the soil of other more glamorous plants. However it came, the plant was first recorded as a garden weed in Craigmillar, Edinburgh, in 1904 and, since the 1930s, has spread at an astonishing rate.

Miniature paragliders

Even in the highest, most remote mountains, New Zealand willowherb can now be found growing on rocks, gravel and among stones in streams and rivers – anywhere in fact that's similar to where it thrives back home in New Zealand. Away from the mountains, it grows on paths, tracks, quarries, banks and as a garden weed. It has a clever secret weapon to help it get about – paragliding is the key to its mobility. Each tiny white flower produces a seed-pod held on a long stalk well above the ground. Once ripe, the pod splits open into four strips, and hundreds of seeds are released. Each seed bears a tuft of long white hairs (a pappus) about eight to ten times as long as the minute 1mm seed. Caught in the wind, especially in the mountains, these seeds can travel for many miles, just like a paraglider, spreading the willowherb far and wide.

ABOVE Once ripe, the seed pod of New Zealand willowherb splits open, releasing its seeds to travel on the wind.

BELOW Carried on swirling mountain air currents, paragliders journey for many miles, probably often accompanied by invisible seeds.

One to watch?

There is a final twist to the willowherb's tale. The vast majority of non-native plants in the British Isles are totally benign, finding their place alongside native species with no ill-effects, which is exactly what the New Zealand willowherb has done. Despite growing in the same areas as some of our rarest plants, such as tufted saxifrage (*S. cespitosa*), it has succeeded in finding its own little place to flourish and has upset no one, until recently, that is. Now, as our winters grow warmer and our mountains see less snow and ice, patches of New Zealand willowherb have grown bigger, stronger and more competitive.

Maybe it is too soon to worry about this little 'fella', but perhaps it's another one for us to keep an eye on, just in case we suddenly find that we have a little thug living on our hills.

For the time being, it's good to marvel at the way the minuscule creeper has managed to spread so far and wide – and so high. It's been discovered growing at least 900m up a Welsh mountain, quite a feat for a tiny plant with a miniature paraglider.

LOOKING TO THE FUTURE

Our uplands and mountains often seem remote, lofty and quiet but, like any other habitat, they're in a constant state of flux. New plants are arriving and old friends leaving all the time. The continuous change on our mountains makes them incredibly exciting places to explore and among the most dramatic spots for plant-hunting.

What of the impact of climate change on upland habitats? It's true that snow lies on the ground less often these days. Our springs are drier and our summers warmer, even on the highest peaks. However, our evidence of earlier cycles of climate change in past millennia suggests that we've seen warmer periods than we're now experiencing, when our alpine plants and lichens survived, much as they still do in the warmer alpine areas of southern Europe.

However, with humans making ever greater demands on the landscape, our mountain plants are possibly under more pressure than ever before. Still, they're incredibly tough little characters that won't give up too easily. If we just give them a chance, allow them to grow, thrive and use their incredible biological survival tricks (see pp.132–3), then our upland plants have every chance of being here for another 10,000 years.

CHAPTER FIVE

OVER THE GARDEN WALL

PREVIOUS PAGE Cottage gardens are beautiful, dynamic places full of growth and change, where plants are left to seed around freely for a relaxed and natural look.

With an estimated 16 million gardens in the British Isles, there's no doubt that our little green plots, along with the multitude of wild things that they harbour, have an important role to play in promoting a healthy balance in nature. Gardens have not only a huge impact on biodiversity, but also a dramatic effect on what's growing across the country as our garden plants increasingly escape into the wild.

Sally, Chris and Trevor peer over a garden wall covered in moss and lichens. Such barriers present no problems for many garden plants, which readily leap to the other side and find a new home in the wild.

Ever since people first started cultivating plants in ancient times, garden species have been jumping over the wall, escaping into the wild from our parks and botanic gardens, from our country estates and backyard plots. As a result, gardening trends and gardeners' tastes have played a tremendous role in shaping the landscape of the British Isles. Today, there are more non-native than native plants growing in the wild – in fact, there are just over 1,500 newcomers compared with 1,400 natives. Most new arrivals have escaped from our gardens and, once out, some find their new homes so comfortable that they become naturalized in the surrounding countryside (see p.29).

For plant detectives, this influx of interesting species adds a touch of the exotic to our islands, but what of their impact on our countryside? Are they killing off the native species and other wild things? Of all the new plants introduced over the years, only eighty-seven – less than 6 per cent of all non-natives – have had a negative ecological impact on native wildlife. Some of these baddies, though, such as New Zealand pigmyweed (*Crassula helmsii*), can cause real damage, often smothering the local vegetation. Arriving here from other countries, with no natural predators to keep them in check, they're usually free to invade and spread. The most successful newcomers, such as rhododendron (*Rhododendron x superponticum*), move in rapidly and fight their corner. Invariably, they've evolved special survival tricks that give them an extra competitive edge, an X-factor in their biology that enables them to dominate. It then becomes a battle between people and plants, with science deployed in the struggle to control the aggressive newcomers. Sometimes, though, they can bring benefits, such as new sources of nectar or pollen for insects. In the grand scheme of things, life is rarely clear-cut. It's the balance of nature that's wonderful.

RHODODENDRON

In 1894, the Victorian botanist Sir Joseph Dalton Hooker jotted down some thoughts on rhododendron in his notebook, speculating that 'Mr. Nightingale's Rhododendron groves …' at Embley in Hampshire, southern England, might be '… more splendid than those found in the Himalayas'. Hooker's simple note appears to be the first record of rhododendron growing in the wild in the British Isles.

Although beautiful in flower, our common rhododendron has spread from gardens and is widely regarded as a pest species in the British Isles. It crowds out native flora and suppresses growth with its dense canopy of leaves.

Beauty or beast?

Since then, our common rhododendron (*R. x superponticum*) has spread to all corners of the British Isles. Did Hooker realize the vigour of the monster that they had on their hands or the effect that it would have on our countryside? Probably not. He certainly couldn't have known that it would play host to an incredible microscopic organism with the power to alter the face of our woodlands, mountains and moorlands forever.

Just a brief glance at the latest distribution maps immediately reveals the scale of the plant's massive increase over the last fifty years (below). The only areas it avoids are the driest, most lime-rich soils on chalk and limestone, preferring damp, acidic soil on sandy heaths and in woodlands where it sneaks in under the forest canopy and slowly fans out. Where the plant really comes into its own, though, is on the mountains in the west – there it spreads out on to moors and rocky hillsides, damp ravines and stream sides, sometimes completely covering the hillsides, which turn a shocking pink-purple in June.

The national distribution maps for rhododendron reveal the sheer scale of its spread across the British Isles over the last fifty years. Today, it is recorded from nearly 70 per cent of all the 10km squares in Britain and Ireland.

RHODODENDRON
RHODODENDRON X SUPERPONTICUM

1962

TODAY

Some people love the plant, especially for the vibrant splash of early-summer colour that it adds to our mountains, lending a touch of the orient to the British landscape at an otherwise rather dull time of year. In reality, though, this plant is a thug and it's having a devastating effect on our wildlife in more ways than one.

The unstoppable super plant

Rhododendron is incredibly well designed for invasion, with four weapons in its biological armoury that can be deployed to muscle out native species and spread across the landscape.

 ### A fast worker

The plant grows quickly and forms an incredibly dense canopy of evergreen leaves, which are held flat in a ring at the tip of each twig. If you were to look down on a rhododendron bush from above, you would see almost no ground visible beneath it. In fact, just 3 per cent of sunlight reaches the ground underneath rhododendron bushes. Almost nothing can survive in such dark conditions – if you were to cut down the spreading branches of a bush, all you'd see would be bare ground beneath because, as the bushes grow, they shade out almost everything in their way.

ABOVE AND BELOW
Rhododendron at
its beautiful worst,
carpeting the hillsides
around Beddgelert in
Snowdonia, North Wales.

FLOWERING TIMES	J	F	M	A	M	J	J	A	S	O	N	D
Rhododendron	✿	✿	✿	✿	✿	✿	✿	✿	✿	✿	✿	✿

Rhododendron pollen contains a toxin called grayanotoxin, which poisons some of the grazing animals that feed on its flowers. People, also, can fall ill if they eat honey made by bees collecting rhododendron pollen. There are even stories from ancient Greece of whole armies having been incapacitated by their indulgence in this 'mad honey'.

 Myriad, fast-reaching seeds

Although our common rhododendron is not native to this country, insects love its flowers and pollinate them profusely. As a result, the amount of seed set can be very high. Each flower pod can produce as many as 7,000 seeds and it is estimated that a large bush can generate up to a million seeds in a season. Small and light, these seeds can travel up to 1km away on the wind, invading new areas far from the parent bush.

 Wide-spreading branches

Rhododendron produces low, spreading branches that often come into contact with the ground. When they do, they invariably root into the soil and produce a vigorous new plant, which grows and spreads out, extending the edge of the bush even further.

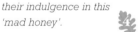 **Self-defensive, poisonous leaves**

As a defence against grazing animals and insects, the plant's leaves produce poisonous chemicals called phenols, which are especially concentrated in young leaves and shoots. As very few insects or animals can tolerate the toxic chemicals in rhododendron leaves, there's nothing to keep the plant in check. As old leaves build up underneath a bush, their poisonous phenols increase in the top layers of the surrounding soil, where they can prevent the seeds of native plants from germinating. (It's widely thought that rhododendron roots also produce a poison to achieve a similar effect, but there's no scientific evidence to prove the theory.)

Ecosystem engineer

Because it modifies its habitat so completely, rhododendron is described as an ecosystem engineer. In effect, it creates an entirely new habitat in which it reigns supreme. When it spreads into woodland, for instance, the trees above a rhododendron bush can carry on growing, but nearly everything beneath perishes – almost nothing survives among its dense, overshadowed thickets. Mosses, liverworts, lichens and fungi are especially sensitive and die quickly, along with the wild things that they support.

Outside the shaded woodlands, on open heaths and moors where the plant can flourish in the sunlight, it grows in even denser stands, smothering the local vegetation. The native heathers, bilberry, mosses and lichens all die beneath its tight thickets. At such times, an advancing front can often be seen (below), with young rhododendrons springing up in the heather behind the frontline of mature bushes.

Today, as a result of the devastating effects of this aggressive plant's presence in vast areas of the British Isles, government agencies, voluntary organizations and landowners are spending a huge amount of money and effort to rid our landscape of the pest (see overleaf). In the Snowdonia National Park alone, complete eradication is estimated at a cost of £10 million.

ABOVE In ten years' time, these seedling rhododendrons will have grown into large bushes, smothering the surrounding heather.

BELOW Almost nothing can grow in the deep shade and leaf litter beneath a mature rhododendron.

Taming the dragon

In a concerted effort to control the rhododendron invasion, two main methods have been deployed with some success.

 ### Slash and burn

Where the shrub grows thick and dense, a 'slash and burn' technique is usually adopted. Every standing trunk and branch is cut down and burnt, leaving a devastated landscape as the shaded ground beneath the bushes is laid bare. The hard graft is often done by volunteers who manage to clear vast areas, but on occasion even the British Army has been called in to tackle the worst sites, such as the Aberglaslyn Pass and Nant Gwynant valley in Snowdonia.

The most important part of the operation occurs immediately afterwards, when each and every sawn-off stump is hand-treated with herbicide. The penetrating effect of the chemical reaches right down into the plant's root systems, killing it off completely. If herbicide isn't applied, every stump and stem on the hillside will quickly re-sprout with incredible energy and, in little more than a few seasons, the plant will return to its former dominance.

After helping to clear a hillside of rhododendron, Trevor, Sally and Chris pile the plant's cut stems onto a bonfire. It will be a decade before the bare, cleared hillside left behind is covered with heather once again.

 Drill and douse

Where the invasion is more like an advancing frontline, with other native plants still growing between the rhododendrons, a different technique is used. Teams of skilled operatives are armed with a battery-powered hand drill and pistol-like injector connected to a back-pack of herbicide; these efficient assassins fight their way to the centre of a bush, drill several holes into its base and inject herbicide into the apertures.

It's a remarkably effective way of dispatching the pest, as herbicide is transported around the entire bush, killing leaves, stems and roots, while nearby plants remain untouched. A few months later, all that's left are dead, grey skeletons on the hillside, while the native bushes that had cowered beneath the rhododendrons rapidly grow back. Amazingly, within a season, hillsides can be transformed by the swift reappearance of native heathland and moorland.

We'll never rid our landscape of rhododendron – quite clearly, it is here to stay, but as long as we can keep it in check and far from our most sensitive and important plant areas (IPAs), perhaps we can learn to live with it (see pp.238–9). After all, it's a brilliant masterpiece of biological engineering – a typically Victorian invention.

A highly infested site can take many hours to clear – every stem has to be cut and then treated with herbicide.

THE TANGLED HISTORY OF RHODODENDRON

Rhododendrons have an exotic and knotted history that has only recently come to light. It's often thought that all rhododendrons come from China. Many do, but not our common rhododendron, which is now spreading across the British Isles. Its origin is somewhat closer to home. In fact, the very first rhododendrons to arrive in the British Isles in the mid eighteenth century came not from China, but from North America and Europe. Gardeners of the time cultivated a small range of three North American species (*R. maximum*, *R. catawbiense* and *R. macrophyllum*) and one European species collected from Spain, Portugal and eastern Europe (*R. ponticum*). It was not until the early nineteenth century that the first exotic rhododendrons came

The two North American species, R. macrophyllum *(above) and* R. catawbiense *(below), and the European species* R. ponticum *(opposite top) were cultivated in Victorian gardens, eventually giving rise to* R. x superponticum *(opposite bottom), seen here invading upland moorland in County Mayo, Ireland.*

from China. More Chinese rhododendrons would appear a century later after the botanist George Forrest organized nine expeditions to Sikkim between 1904 and 1930. By then, the European and North American species were already being cultivated and cross-bred in British gardens.

A Frankenstein of Victorian creation
Unlike the European species, the three North American ones were extremely hardy and able to withstand hard winter frosts. They also produced many more flowers, so gardeners did what gardeners always do in these circumstances – they crossed the four species together to create a range of hybrids. From the offspring, they selected the best, most vigorous and prolific and grew these on, re-crossing and selecting the best again. Little did they know it at the time, but the Victorians were breeding a monster.

Nineteenth-century gardeners loved the new rhododendron (then known by the humble name *R. ponticum*), because it was so easy to grow and spread quickly. Magnificent in flower, it became a 'must have' species and was planted in huge quantities. In gardens, estates and country houses all over the British Isles, '*R. ponticum*' filled the borders and shrubberies. Escape over the garden wall was inevitable, although it didn't happen from just one place, but rather from all over the country simultaneously, causing a sudden pervasive spread.

This detailed history of our common rhododendron was only unravelled in 2011. Until then, we thought that the plant growing in the wild in the British Isles was the pure European species, *R. ponticum*. Now we know that it's a hybrid between *R. ponticum* and the three North American species. In a reference, perhaps to the most unstoppable of American superheroes, it's now been renamed *R. x superponticum*.

RHODODENDRON DÉJÀ VU

When non-native rhododendrons were shipped to the British Isles in the mid eighteenth century (see pp.166–7), it was not the first time that they had visited our shores.

Ice Age rhododendron

Long before the first hunter-gatherers had even set foot in the British Isles in the wake of the retreating ice sheets, *c*.8000 BC, *R. ponticum* had flourished here during the last Ice Age, which began *c*.2.58 million years ago. In cycles spanning thousands of years, glaciers advanced and retreated across the globe. During the warmer interglacial periods, different plants came and went. As they flourished, their pollen settled in lakes and bogs, where they were eventually preserved in peat deposits, leaving us tantalizing clues.

Prehistoric pollen

Incredibly, pollen grains of *R. ponticum* have been found preserved in Irish peat deposits that date from between 424,000 to 374,000 years ago, during what's known as the Hoxnian interglacial. So, hundreds of

Pollen grains of R. ponticum *are coated in tough sporopollenin, a polymer resistant to rot.*

thousands of years before the arrival of the first modern Britons, *R. ponticum* had made itself at home in our green islands.

The next advance of the ice sheets, spreading down from the poles and extending all the way to southern Britain, pushed the warm-loving plant away forever. For some reason, it never returned – at least not until we brought it back from Europe thousands of years later and used it to breed *R. x superponticum* (see pp.166–7).

Doubly deadly

There's more than one twist to the rhododendron story, however. The super plant is a double murderer. Not only does it behave like a monster in its own right by wreaking diabolical havoc on our landscape, but it also acts as the perfect host to a deadly new disease that could change the look of our countryside forever.

In 2002, the fungus-like organism *Phytophthora ramorum* was first reported in the British Isles. Closely related to the potato blight that brought devastation to Ireland during the Great Famine (1845–52), which forced many Irish families to emigrate to North America, this new blight appears to have taken the return journey and arrived here from the USA. *P. ramorum* probably came across on container-grown nursery plants, as the blight was first found infecting a viburnum (*Viburnum tinus*) in a garden centre and quickly spread to gardens and nurseries. Like the potato blight, this disease has the potential to change the face of the countryside, and its increase in the wild is being helped by rhododendron.

P. ramorum usually kills the trees it infects. The name Sudden Oak Death refers to the effect it's had on trees in North America, especially tanoaks (*Notholithocarpus densiflorus*), although they're not so much oaks as evergreen trees in the beech family (*Fagaceae*). In the British Isles, beech trees (*Fagus sylvatica*) are mostly affected, but the fungus is also found on horse chestnut (*Aesculus hippocastanum*), sweet chestnut (*Castanea sativa*), our native oak species (*Quercus* sp.) and sycamore (*Acer pseudoplatanus*). Infected trees develop bleeding cankers (open wounds) on their trunks, which ooze a thick, dark sap. Although the sap contains billions of *P. ramorum*'s infectious spores, fortunately it tends simply to run down the trunk rather than spreading to other trees.

An infected rhododendron, though, can play a deadly role. Being such a tough plant, it's not actually killed by *P. ramorum*, but can survive with the infestation and produce infectious leaves for a long time, up to ten years. On the surface of its leaves, millions of spores are produced, which infect neighbouring bushes and plants whenever it rains and the spores get splashed around. Worse still, where infected thickets of rhododendrons occur in dense stands on uplands and heathlands, they act like a superconnected highway, allowing *P. ramorum* to spread much further than it otherwise could.

BELOW LEFT Chris inspects a weeping canker on the bark of a larch infected by P. ramorum.

BELOW CENTRE Infection by P. ramorum *usually leads to brown lesions and a soft, wilted appearance.*

BELOW RIGHT P. ramorum's *reproductive zoospores (spores capable of swimming) use a propeller-like flagellum to move through water when infecting new trees.*

Chris prepares to take to the air in a survey for P. ramorum. Air patrols are the fastest and most effective way to search for new outbreaks in the thousands of hectares of forest now at risk of infection. A survey by air also reduces the possibility of ground surveyors transferring the disease from one forest to another.

New lines of attack

Like all the most virulent diseases, however, *P. ramorum* is now altering its line of attack, switching hosts and finding yet more species to infect. In January 2009, it was found for the first time in bilberry (*Vaccinium myrtillus*) at a site in Staffordshire. Bilberry (known as blaeberry in Scotland and llus in Wales) covers vast areas of western Britain and Ireland, providing shelter and food for a wide range of wildlife. If *P. ramorum* continues to infect this shrub and spreads on a national scale, the character and ecology of our heathlands, mountains and moorlands could change forever.

Just a year later, in 2010, *P. ramorum* evolved again and spread from rhododendron into Japanese larch (*Larix kaempferi*), one of the most important forestry trees in the British Isles. The fungus then started behaving differently. Up until then, none of the infected forest trees, such as beech, had produced any spores on their leaves. On Japanese larch, however, the fungus not only produces spores on the tree's leaves, but generates five times as many as on rhododendron bushes. What's worrying is that the spores pour out from the larch's high tree crowns on to the surrounding countryside, massively increasing the potential for further spread.

The forestry agencies have taken immediate action, conducting aerial surveys to monitor outbreaks, and felling infected trees. By the end of 2011, 3 million larch trees had been cut down, mainly in southwest England and South Wales where the wetter, milder climate seems to suit the fungus. What's now clear is that most of the sites with affected larch trees also contain infected rhododendron, demonstrating the role played by rhododendron in the spread of the disease.

Organisms such as *P. ramorum* are obviously very clever, as they constantly evolve, taking whatever opportunities they can to adapt and to exploit the plants that they infect. In 2012, infected larch trees were found for the first time in Sussex and Surrey, in southeast England – well outside the earlier outbreak areas in western Britain, showing how quickly this disease is spreading. Both sites were close to infected rhododendrons. Although this blight is microscopic, its impact could be incredible. As always, the most important thing is to keep watching the situation carefully.

An outbreak site in South Wales, where infected Japanese larch trees were felled in 2011, leaving behind a devastated landscape that can no longer be replanted with larch. If all our larches become infected, this could be the fate of 5 per cent of the total wooded area of the British Isles.

Three innocents

Of the 1,500 non-native species that have escaped from gardens into the wild, the majority, at least 1,400, are completely benign and not thugs like rhododendron (see pp.159–71). After flourishing in our gardens, they eventually escape into the wild and nestle in among the native vegetation, causing little harm. Most, in fact, add not only colour, but also contrast and variety to the landscape. If anything, they even increase the delights of searching for wild plants, as there are always new ones to look out for and you never quite know what you'll find next. The three non-natives here are among the most widespread of our innocent newcomers.

Ivy-leaved toadflax

Recorded from the wild as early as 1640, the creeping ivy-leaved toadflax (*Cymbalaria muralis*) from the mountains of Europe is now common on walls and pavements – almost every mortared wall seems to have a patch. It spreads by seed or from fragments of its rooting stems.

Pineappleweed

Having escaped from Kew Gardens in Surrey, England, in 1871, pineappleweed (*Matricaria discoidea*) has become one of the fastest-spreading plants in the British Isles. Almost every field gateway and farmyard has a mat of this plant and it now flourishes on roadsides, waste ground and along tracks. Its small seeds are mainly spread on soil that's got stuck to tyres.

American willowherb

One of our most frequently occurring non-native plants, American willowherb (*Epilobium ciliatum*) from North America was first recorded in the wild in 1891 and spread rapidly from the 1930s. It's a rather weedy little thing that grows in any disturbed soil, in gardens and felled woodland, on waste ground, walls and pavements. Its tiny seeds, each with a feathery parachute, are wind-borne.

BUDDLEJA

The Victorians loved new things. During the nineteenth century, plant-hunters and explorers scoured the British empire and beyond for novel and exciting species with which to fill their gardens and impress their neighbours. Unfortunately, although many of their finds were beautiful, some turned out to be beasts, just like rhododendron. Another three legendary pests have wreaked similar havoc: buddleja (*Buddleia davidii*), Japanese knotweed (*Fallopia japonica*) and Himalayan balsam (*Impatiens glandulifera*).

Buddleja, a beautiful woody shrub with purple flower spikes, excited much interest among Victorian gardeners. Discovered in China in the nineteenth century, it was described as growing in luxuriant thickets, providing 'excellent harbourage to tigers'. After such a write-up, the first buddlejas to arrive on our shores in the 1890s seemed rather sickly by comparison, prompting expeditions to find

Buddleja's spikes of purple flowers produced in summer are richly scented and full of nectar, attracting butterflies and bees (inset). The distribution maps for the plant reveal the scale of its spread across the British Isles in the last fifty years.

BUDDLEJA
BUDDLEIA DAVIDII

1962

TODAY

ABOVE Buddleja is now a very familiar plant on walls, particularly in urban areas. Its roots have an ability to penetrate cracks in brickwork and concrete and, as the bushes grow, they swell causing extensive damage to these structures.

more vigorous plants. What the explorers brought back was certainly vigorous, rather more so than anyone had intended.

Over the course of the next century, buddleja was planted widely across the country. As the plant produces large quantities of wind-borne seed, it wasn't long before it escaped from gardens. First recorded growing in the wild in Gwynedd, North Wales, in 1922, it was then reported in Middlesex in 1927. For several decades, until the 1970s, buddleja crept out from gardens steadily but slowly. Something then changed and it began spreading rapidly, moving out into the countryside, taking over railways and springing up in pavement cracks, on city walls, building sites and waste ground. The shift in its behaviour seems to be related to climate change. In our milder winters, buddleja seeds germinate more readily and more seedlings survive and grow to maturity. As a result, the plant is now found practically everywhere in lowland Britain and Ireland.

Is the spread of the plant a problem? It depends on who you are. For the train companies, clearing buddleja from tracks and embankments each year is a recurrent battle that costs hundreds of thousands of pounds. For conservationists, the jury is still out. On the one hand, buddleja is great news for declining butterflies and moths, providing a valuable source of nectar in an otherwise flower-poor landscape. Another plus for conservationists is that buddleja hasn't yet made much headway into our wildlife-rich sites, apart from some abandoned chalk pits and quarries, where it can shade-out rare, ground-dwelling insects, bugs and mosses.

On the other hand, in much of the country, buddleja is a botanical thug that grows into the dense thickets so beloved by tigers in China and, unlike our native flowering plants, such as bird's-foot trefoil (*Lotus corniculatus*), it provides no source of food for the caterpillars of butterflies. Perhaps, rather than supporting the spread of a fast-food nectar-fix for butterflies, we should be encouraging more of our own native wildflowers to flourish to ensure that butterflies and other insects have a complete diet throughout their entire lives.

OPPOSITE TOP Arching sprays of broad, heart-shaped leaves made Japanese knotweed a favourite of Victorian gardeners.

JAPANESE KNOTWEED

Another introduction from the Far East, Japanese knotweed (*Fallopia japonica*) was a favourite with Victorian gardeners, who admired its elegant arching branches, deemed worthy of gracing any herbaceous border. The plant's stems are certainly elegant and would indeed add style to any garden, just so long as its borders are the size of a small English county.

In its native home, Japanese knotweed is a scrawling, somewhat battered plant that grows on the exposed slopes of volcanoes. In our damp, mild climate, however, where it has no natural enemies to nibble and feast on its leaves and shoots, the knotweed runs amok. Although the stems die back to ground level each winter, they erupt from the soil in spring, reaching 3m tall by high summer, when they form impenetrable thickets.

Japanese knotweed (inset) has spread in the last fifty years to occupy 75 per cent of the 10km squares mapped in the British Isles (bottom right).

JAPANESE KNOTWEED
FALLOPIA JAPONICA

1962

TODAY

The aerial (above-ground) stems of Japanese knotweed are so tough that they can emerge through the smallest of cracks in tarmac, concrete and masonry, causing considerable damage. Growth rates of up to 4cm a day have been recorded.

A hidden life

What's remarkable for a species that's made such an inroad into our countryside is that it all stems from a single, original plant that was introduced to the British Isles in 1825. Quite simply, every Japanese knotweed today is a genetically identical clone of the original nineteenth-century plant. What's just as astonishing is that the parent plant was female, which means that all Japanese knotweeds in the country are female, so cannot produce any male pollen to generate seed for the next generation. How does the plant spread at all?

Its secret lies underground, where a stem called a rhizome spreads beneath the soil, forming a tangled, branching mass that can reach 3m deep and 7m across. If the smallest rhizome fragments, just 3cm long, are transported to another site, they can grow into a new plant with strong aerial (above-ground) stems that spring up from the underground rhizome. So the weed often grows wherever the rhizome fragments can be easily transported, especially downstream along rivers, but also wherever the soil has been disturbed, as on newly constructed roads and railway banks, around docks, building sites and rubbish tips. The power of the aerial stems to push up through tarmac and to penetrate through cracks in concrete and masonry is the secret of the plant's invincibility. Dense thickets can block drains, damage foundations and walls, and even appear inside buildings.

Tackling the mother of all weeds

Is this weed a major threat to our native plants and wildlife? With its reputation for monopolizing space and shouldering aside other wild things, Japanese knotweed is a menace that we should watch very carefully. Most of the damage done by the plant currently occurs in urban areas, especially in South Wales where it grows on redeveloped coal mines, building sites and new developments. Out in the countryside, too, it can be a big problem for native wildlife, which doesn't stand a chance once the weed gets a grip on a stretch of land, such as a sea cliff or roadside verge. Although it's not that common in totally undeveloped and isolated areas, streams and rivers are still vulnerable in such spots.

To check its spread, severe controls have been put in place. It's illegal to sell Japanese knotweed or transport soil known to contain rhizome fragments. The plant's reputation as the 'mother of all weeds' means that in many areas the authorities are working hard to tackle its spread. Herbicide is one option, but Japanese knotweed is a tough customer. Repeated applications are needed over several years to weaken and kill the plant. If the treatment isn't properly carried out, the strength of the underground rhizome slowly builds and the weed returns at full-throttle after just a few years. Controlling the plant is clearly a time-consuming and expensive process, costing an estimated £166 million a year, with complete eradication priced at £1.5 billion.

A natural cure

As an alternative to chemical warfare, a remarkable biological agent has been deployed. It's the tiny psyllid bug (*Aphalara itadori*), which lives in Japan, where it sucks the sap of Japanese knotweed, reducing its vigour. After extensive testing to ensure that this little Japanese bug doesn't attack any of our native wild plants or crops, it was deemed safe to release in the British Isles in 2010. Trials are ongoing and we've yet to see just how effective the bug will be, but it's incredible to think that, for this most aggressive of invaders, we've had to turn back to mother nature for a solution.

BELOW The juvenile nymphs of the psyllid bug, just 2mm long, suck the sap of Japanese knotweed, reducing its ability to grow and spread.

BOTTOM Japanese knotweed can be a real problem, its dense thickets shading out native vegetation along rivers and in woodland.

GARDEN WALL LICHENS

Garden walls offer some of the most interesting lichen-hunting territory of all. Down at the bottom of the garden, these vertical rock faces provide a quiet place where lichens can grow freely but few other organisms can survive. Often the lichens that live here, such as *Parmelia saxatalis*, grow back-to-back with their neighbours, creating the most beautiful natural mosaics. Just try looking for a lichen-free patch – you might be searching for quite a while, especially on older walls. These seemingly static patterns, made up of diverse shapes and interesting textures, harbour a rainbow of colours that has inspired many an artist. Rather than being simply picturesque scenes, though, these mosaics indicate a dynamic battlefield where lichens jostle for space and light.

Lung lichen (Lobaria pulmonaria) was traditionally thought to be a cure for lung complaints and is still used in herbal medicines today.

Old stone walls harbour a myriad of wild things, which jostle for space and light among their dark crannies.

The slow growth and longevity of lichens, many of which live for hundreds of years, make it difficult to determine the shifting shapes of individual plots and it's certainly true that some lichen boundaries don't change even over very long timescales. Other species, however, have all sorts of tricks up their sleeves, allowing them, over time, to oust a neighbour and grow in its place; to build up dense walls between each

other; or sometimes to grow over the next-door lichen. Whoever said that good neighbours make good friends?

Among these mosaics, the battle isn't confined simply to rival lichens. Individual species also have to defend themselves against bacterial and fungal attack, as well as herbivorous invertebrates, such as slugs, snails and mites. Living for many hundreds of years can be a great advantage, but not if every so often a snail decides to stop for a snack. Fortunately, lichens are equipped with various defensive mechanisms, including chemicals designed to deter their predators. Called 'secondary compounds' or 'lichen substances' (see pp.82–3), these defensive chemicals include antibiotics to fight bacterial infection; anti-fungal compounds to prevent fungal attack; and pesticides to deter snails and other invertebrates from getting their way.

Scientists today are trying to isolate these chemicals, as it's thought that they could be hugely important in the fight against disease. Early people, in fact, used lichens to treat a variety of illnesses. Lung lichen (*Lobaria pulmonaria*), for example, was thought to alleviate chest infections.

The chemicals produced by lichens have also been used to make cloth dyes and perfumes. The Romans, for instance, extracted lichen pigments to dye their togas, favouring *Roccella* for its purple colour, which was worn by emperors. Closer to home, in Scotland, the lichen *Parmelia saxatalis*, sometimes called 'crottle', was scraped off rocks to create dyes for Scottish and Irish tweed, including the famous Burberry and Harris.

Sally discovers some stone-loving lichens on the garden wall (below). The common rock lichen Parmelia saxatalis (below left) was traditionally used in Scotland to create a rich red-brown dye for tweed.

HIMALAYAN BALSAM

Himalayan balsam (*Impatiens glandulifera*) was introduced to our shores as an ornamental garden plant in 1839. At that time, its large exotic flowers were likened to orchids but, unlike orchids, which could cost hundreds of pounds, Himalayan balsam could be obtained for as little as a packet of seed. As it could also be easily cultivated in the garden, it was promoted as a plant that would grow to 'Herculean proportions' with 'splendid invasiveness', which it certainly has. As a measure of its ability to spread quickly, the plant got out into the wild just sixteen years after its arrival in the British Isles and has never looked back. Dense stands of Himalayan balsam now line many river and canal banks in Britain and Ireland. It also invades damp pastures, roadside verges and the edges of lakes, ponds and reed beds.

Unlike most invasive species, Himalayan balsam is an annual, growing from a seed each spring and dying completely in the winter.

HIMALAYAN BALSAM
IMPATIENS GLANDULIFERA

1962

TODAY

This doesn't mean that it lacks impact – in fact, it's the tallest annual in the British Isles, growing more than 2m high and often shading out some of our aggressive native vegetation, such as nettles (*Urtica dioica*).

Famously, the plant's seed pods are its main means of spreading. Once ripe, tensions build up within the pod tissue as different parts grow at varying speeds. Eventually the pod explodes, scattering seed up to 7m away – a process aptly described as ballistic dispersal. You only have to touch a ripe pod to see it erupt, with seeds bursting out at top speed.

A source of controversy

Himalayan balsam has provoked controversy in several areas of conservation. Firstly, it's opened debate about the recent environmental policy of fencing off river banks in order to prevent soil erosion. Once riversides had been sectioned off, Himalayan balsam was observed spreading dramatically in some areas, as the grazing animals that used to feed on the plant were now prevented from reaching the river's edge. Secondly, the plant is much loved by bee-keepers, as its flowers provide a huge amount of pollen, prompting some people to scatter the seed freely in the countryside in an effort to encourage a late summer supply of pollen, which inevitably augments the spread of Himalayan balsam. Thirdly, arguments rage over whether the plant actually causes a problem for native vegetation

ABOVE LEFT A marsh swamped by rampant Himalayan balsam after the removal of the grazing livestock that used to keep the plant in check.

ABOVE The seed pods of Himalayan balsam are formed from five segments that explode like coiled springs, firing the seeds up to 7m away.

OPPOSITE TOP Himalayan balsam flowers come in all shades, from dark pink to pure white.

OPPOSITE Since its escape from British gardens in 1855, Himalayan balsam has spread at an astonishing rate of 645 km^2 per year. The increase in just the last fifty years is clear from the distribution maps.

and wildlife or not. Many contend that it doesn't, pointing to evidence showing that invaded riversides rarely lose plant species or insects. Other conservationists regard the plant as an ecosystem modifier, which completely changes the subtle ecology and balance of the species within a site. The jury might still be out on this one, but so is Himalayan balsam, spreading explosively around the countryside.

NEW ZEALAND PIGMYWEED

One of the fastest-spreading plants in the British Isles today, New Zealand pigmyweed is now ninety times more common than it was fifty years ago. What will its map look like in another fifty years?

We can't blame the Victorians for introducing all the invasive weeds to our islands. Modern ease of travel and access to new plants in garden centres over the last fifty years has enabled gardeners to grow more plants than ever before. Some have had a huge impact on our natural world. One notorious Tasmanian newcomer is New Zealand pigmyweed (*Crassula helmsii*), first innocently introduced in 1911 as a fashionable novelty plant for garden ponds. More recently, during the 1980s and 1990s, it sold in huge quantities after

NEW ZEALAND PIGMYWEED
CRASSULA HELMSII

1962

TODAY

being marketed as the perfect oxygenating plant to keep ponds clean and healthy. On face value, New Zealand pigmyweed certainly seems like the ideal garden pond species. As its name implies, the weed is minute and appears rather inoffensive, with narrow leaves and small flowers, set on a low cushion of thin stems. You'd be forgiven for thinking that it would look great in your pond, but beware – it's often the quiet ones that cause the problems.

Within a few months of the weed being widely planted during the 1980s, garden ponds became completely choked. Spreading through the water and out on to the damp pond edges, it even grew upwards, forming billowing mounds and hummocks of intertwined shoots, so that no open water – let alone any other plants or wildlife – remained visible. Faced with such a thug in their gardens, many people ripped it up and threw it on to the compost heap. We now know that this is the worst way to tackle the problem, as the thin stems get broken up and thousands of fragments are left floating. It's these tiny fragments, some no more than 5mm

BELOW Although the tiny flowers of New Zealand pigmyweed are freely produced, no viable seed is set and reproduction in the British Isles is entirely vegetative (asexual).

BOTTOM New Zealand pigmyweed occupies the flood zone around lake edges, forming dense mats in both the shallow water and along the damp margins.

long, that perpetuate the problem. If even the smallest fragment has just one pair of leaves, it can start a new plant and, within weeks, ponds can become choked again.

A long-distance traveller

Not only that, but these tiny fragments can move far and wide very easily. It takes just one innocent dabbling duck to transfer fragments from one pond to another. On the back of a vole, on the coat of a dog, on the sole of a wellington boot – pigmyweed has found countless ways of getting around. From garden ponds, it quickly escaped into the wild. As early as 1956, it was recorded growing in a pond at Greensted in Essex and has since moved on to lakes, reservoirs, ditches and slow-flowing canals. Clearly, this is no ordinary little chap – in fact, it's proving to be unstoppable. After fifty-six years in the wild, it now grows in nearly a third of all the hectads mapped out on the national distribution maps. What's worrying is that it's proving to be just as aggressive in the wild as it was in gardens – smothering all native pond vegetation and thereby diminishing food and oxygen for insects and fish. Unfortunately, the weed grows particularly well in the seasonal heathland pools that develop in warm and wet areas, such as the New Forest in Hampshire, southern England. Its arrival here is especially bad news for the local pondlife, as such pools are home to an incredibly rich diversity of rare wild things, which won't stand a chance in the face of the newcomer. To stop it in its tracks, we need to understand the secret of its success.

A hyperactive metabolism

A clue to the weed's success lies in its metabolism – like a hyperactive teenager, it simply never stops. Endowed with the special Crassulacean Acid Metabolism (CAM), it's almost always growing. The weed's CAM is connected to its ability to photosynthesize – the process by which plants absorb daytime sunlight to produce the glucose and other sugars that fuel the majority of life on earth (see p.43). Photosynthesis can only occur when carbon dioxide is present, which most plants take in only during the day. New Zealand Pigmyweed, though, can absorb carbon dioxide at night as well, storing the extra quota in a special organic acid within its cells until photosynthesis can occur in the sunlight. During the day the plant's supply of stored carbon dioxide is then released, allowing more photosynthesis to take place and for a longer time. The result is that New Zealand pigmyweed can assimilate carbon

A flock of common teal in flight over Elmley Marshes on the Isle of Sheppey in Kent, southeast England. This species of duck feeds in sheltered wetlands by dabbling for plants and, in so doing, helps the spread of native and non-native species. In winter it migrates in large flocks to Africa and South Asia.

dioxide for twenty-four hours a day, every day of the year, with no dormant period during the winter. Day or night, spring or winter, pigmyweed just keeps on growing.

Weeding out the weed

With ponds and lakes getting choked up with the weed, a variety of desperate measures have been taken to stop its spread:

Covering ponds in thick black plastic

Blocking out the light should, in principle, kill the plant, but New Zealand pigmyweed can go into a state of suspended animation, only to start growing again when the light returns. For the 'black-out' to work, ponds need to be kept in the dark for at least six months to ensure that the plant has died.

Freezing the pond with liquid nitrogen

Liquid nitrogen is a cryogenic fluid, which causes rapid freezing on contact with living tissue. When the fluid is poured into a pond, its dry-ice effects can be dramatic, but it only seems to freeze the top layer of plant growth with which it comes into contact. Deep below the surface, nothing freezes and the weed recovers.

Flooding sites with salty sea water

An extreme and expensive measure, flooding the pond with sea water takes time and, of course, can only be done by the coast.

Dousing the weed with herbicides

Herbicidal control is the most successful method, but any use of herbicides in water bodies in the wild needs careful control, has consequences for other wildlife and is expensive.

Infilling ponds with soil

Although infilling is perhaps the most popular method for smaller ponds, it is fairly dramatic and expensive, as a new pond has to be dug elsewhere.

New Zealand pigmyweed quickly colonizes sites, not only choking native vegetation, such as marsh pennywort (Hydrocotyle vulgaris) here, but also altering water chemistry and lowering water oxygen levels. In small ponds, this can have serious consequences for fish and invertebrates.

New Zealand pigmyweed is a particular problem in the New Forest in Hampshire, southern England, where it smothers seasonal pools that are home to rare species, such as yellow centaury. It is carried between ponds on the hooves of grazing animals, whose footprints can be seen here.

New Zealand pigmyweed is clearly here to stay. With a biology unlike that of almost any other plant in the British Isles and with a frightening ability to survive and move around, this long-distance traveller remains one of our fastest-spreading plants. Its impact on our native wildlife is huge, but there's little that can be done to stop it now. All we can do is to clear it from our most important wildlife-rich sites and, crucially, we can stop planting it in our gardens from where yet more of the weed can escape into the wild.

At garden centres, we should think twice about what we're buying and the damage that it might wreak on the countryside. New Zealand pigmyweed's merits as a pond plant are really quite limited – on balance, it's a rather dull little weed, with practically no attractive qualities, yet it could well destroy your garden pond.

THE GARDENER'S CODE

Gardeners have a responsibility to ensure that invasive species don't escape into the wild. To help raise awareness of the issues involved, Horticultural Codes of Practice have been developed in England, Wales and Scotland by various governments, trade associations, horticultural bodies and environmental organizations. The codes are designed to highlight the problems that invasive non-natives can cause and to advise anyone involved in horticulture what basic steps can be taken to minimize the impact of invasive plants.

Dispose of plant waste responsibly – never fly-tip. Fly-tipping is illegal and unnecessary, as much waste can be composted or passed to municipal recycling centres. Particular care should be taken to ensure that aquatic plants do not end up in watercourses, such as rivers and ponds.

Know exactly what you are buying and growing. Avoid growing plants known to be invasive. Consider alternatives and, when growing native plants, use those of local origin if possible. Don't pass on the problem: think about a non-native's invasive potential when you exchange plants with friends, or grow species from seeds.

Take advice on the best control techniques. Invasive plants can be difficult to control, but timely action will reduce the scale of the problem. For species such as buddleja, which spread by seed, dead-heading after flowering will help (see pp.173–4). For

plants with strong rhizome systems, such as Japanese knotweed, root-barriers can be used to contain their spread (see pp.175–7).

Control invasive non-native plants safely. Care should be taken when using herbicides and machinery, particularly near water. Manufacturers' instructions and recommendations on mixing and applying herbicides should always be followed. Although the range of herbicides available to the amateur gardener is limited, any guidance on safe use still applies.

Be aware of relevant legislation. Legislation on non-natives and their safe control and disposal should be followed at all times. You should keep abreast of the updated lists of plants that are illegal to spread in the wild, such as montbretia (*Crocosmia x crocosmiiflora*) and three-cornered garlic (*Allium triquetrum*).

Both three-cornered garlic (below) and montbretia (bottom) call for safe disposal to prevent their spread.

Three to watch

It's always best to nip a problem in the bud. For many of our most invasive species, such as rhododendron, they're now so common in the wild that control is almost impossible (see pp.159–71). Today the emphasis is rather on spotting the next invaders before they become uncontrollable. The three here are worth watching carefully.

Tree-of-heaven

Native to China, where it supports the ailanthus silkmoth, the tree-of-heaven (*Ailanthus altissima*) was first recorded in the wild in 1935. As it tolerates high levels of pollution, it's now widely planted in towns and cities. A fast-growing tree, it can reach heights of 15m in just twenty-five years but it's also short-lived, rarely surviving more than fifty years. The tree hasn't often set seed in the British Isles, but spreads aggressively by suckering, whereby new shoots spring up around the parent plant from its roots. It has become an invasive species due to its ability to suppress the germination of competitive plants with the toxic chemical ailanthone, which is released from its roots. Across the world the tree-of-heaven is such a highly invasive species that in some places, such as North America, it's now nicknamed the tree-from-hell. If our climate continues to warm up, this one could become a real pest.

Winter primrose

Although this pretty relative of the evening primrose (*Oenothera* sp.) has been sold as an ideal pond plant, it can choke and smother everything in its path (above). Only recently introduced to our islands from North America, water primrose (*Ludwigia grandiflora*) was first recorded in the wild in 1999, but it's now been spotted at about eleven sites. Its potential impact is so great that it's illegal to introduce the plant into the wild, and any infestations elicit a Rapid Response Protocol for immediate eradication by herbicide and dredging.

Giant rhubarb

Introduced from western South America in 1849, this gigantic rhubarb (*Gunnera tinctoria*) is popular in gardens, where its massive leaves expand to more than 1m across (above). It's also spreading in the wild but is highly invasive, destroying ecosystems and even killing willow trees. Herbicide and mechanical digging can control it but, with each flower producing over 250,000 seeds, eradication is a long, hard battle.

LOOKING TO THE FUTURE

Gardens offer wonderful havens for wild things. With their mix of native species growing alongside exotic varieties from around the world, they provide a valuable refuge for bugs, butterflies, bees, birds and all manner of other wildlife. We must not forget the wider countryside, though, especially as we seem to be losing our former easy association with wild species. Even the names of everyday wildflowers, such as cowslip (*Primula veris*), once familiar to previous generations, are now being forgotten. Maybe if we learnt a bit more about our native plants and discovered their individual stories, we'd be better able to appreciate their qualities again, which is the ethos behind Plantlife's Grow Wild campaign. It's an innovative programme that encourages everyone to cultivate native plants in the garden, where they can be touched, smelled and enjoyed, enabling us to recognize and value the very same flowers when we encounter them in the wild.

With so many fresh and unfamiliar species escaping into the wild today, we never quite know what we'll stumble on next. The multicultural newcomers can be exciting, adding colour and interest to habitats across the country, but we do need to be careful and ward off the trouble-makers. The only way to do so is to keep a close eye on all the plants around us, no matter where they come from. It's certainly an exciting and important time to get out there and really discover what an incredible range of wild things our islands have to offer.

Plantlife's Grow Wild garden of 2006 showed that native plants can take centre stage in modern, contemporary designs.

WILDFLOWERS IN THE GARDEN

It can be surprising just how many garden favourites are actually native British species. The beautiful pasqueflower (*Pulsatilla vulgaris*), scented chamomile (*Chamaemelum nobile*), evergreen box (*Buxus sempervirens*), deep blue jacob's-ladder (*Polemonium caeruleum*), fragrant lily-of-the-valley (*Convallaria majalis*) and pretty cornflower (*Centaurea cyanus*) (right) originate in the wild. Unfortunately, though, they're all now either threatened or declining and need our protection in the wild.

GARDENING ON THE WILD SIDE

The world of show gardens can sometimes be a rather formal environment of high design and competition glamour, but however varied the brief or the competition theme, Chris Myers' designs invariably capture a little piece of the wild. From his rummaging around the countryside, he always brings back over the garden wall some wild things to showcase in his gardens.

Waterscape.com Garden
BBC Gardeners' World Live 2004
RHS GOLD MEDAL AND BEST IN SHOW

This rustic, waterside garden earned Chris his first-ever RHS Gold Medal and also the honour of being awarded 'Best in Show' (below). Sponsored by British Waterways, the picturesque design even included a life-size canal as its centrepiece. With its rural and water-based themes, Chris's garden was designed to generate interest in the recreational activities enjoyed on and around British canals.

Yorkshire Forward's At a Dale's Pace
RHS Flower Show at Tatton Park 2005
SILVER GILT MEDAL

A garden close to Chris's heart, this lush, leafy plot was inspired by his home turf and the experience of outdoor work (above). The design highlighted Yorkshire Forward's two initiatives, Growing Routes and Bright Spark, both aimed at helping the young and anyone with rural skills to establish their own businesses. More than 100,000 visitors attended the show and many more television viewers admired Chris's garden.

The Bodgery
sponsored by Vertibax
BBC Gardeners' World Live 2011
RHS GOLD MEDAL AND BEST IN SHOW
FAÇADE GARDEN

With this small but perfectly formed garden, Chris managed to bring a bit of the wild into the formal setting of a garden design competition (above). His contribution showcased the designer's passion for wild plants, as well as his knowledge of bodgery, a form of traditional wood-working from the trees of the forest. Fairly packed with authentic details inspired by the big wild backyard that Chris has spent so many years exploring, his bodgery patch even included a rabbit hole and a bodger at work alongside a hand-crafted wooden hut.

The Ricola Garden
of Natural Goodness
BBC Gardeners' World Live 2009
RHS GOLD MEDAL

Inspired by the herbal-sweet manufacturer Ricola, this wonderfully fresh and verdant garden showcased all thirteen herbs used in their recipes. Reminiscent of leafy high alpine passes, the garden even featured its very own alpine-style hut.

Edibly Unkempt
RHS Hampton Court Palace Flower Show 2009
SHOW FEATURE

Commissioned by the Royal Horticultural Society (RHS) on behalf of the Mayor of London Boris Johnson, Chris's Edibly Unkempt urban design (below) was one of three gardens and six balconies exhibited at

the *Edible Spaces with Capital Growth* event held at the Hampton Court Palace Flower Show in 2009. The initiative, launched by Boris Johnson and Rosie Boycott of London Food, was intended to show city dwellers that anyone can grow food, no matter how small their outside space. The exhibited gardens were full of practical and innovative ideas to inspire Londoners. Chris's design, for instance, included edible flowers, as well as nutritious vegetables and herbs.

CHAPTER SIX
FARMLANDS

PREVIOUS PAGE Poppies, such as long-headed poppy here (Papaver dubium), have long been icons of our farmed landscape. As they decline, new crops such as blue Phacelia (Phacelia tanacetifolia) become more frequent.

There are 17.2 million hectares of farmland in the British Isles, equivalent to around 43 million football pitches, which amounts to about 70 per cent of the entire country. Although we import 31 million tonnes of food per year to feed a growing population, the demand on our home farmlands is still immense. Every year we produce more than 20 million tonnes of cereals, 13,174 million litres of milk, 15 million lambs and 1.6 million beef cattle.

Where did it all start? Around 7,500 years ago, the early hunter-gatherers who had arrived in the British Isles in the wake of the retreating ice sheets began clearing the native wildwood to settle down and farm the land. In the newly created fields, they sowed edible grain, such as emmer wheat (*Triticum dicoccum*) and six-row barley (*Hordeum hexastichum*), and grazed captive animals including ancient cattle. This type of mixed farming created a fantastic variety of habitats in which animals and plants could thrive, adapting to the opportunities provided by their new homes.

Since the early days of farming, many more man-made habitats have gradually been developed for agriculture, ranging from hedges to ditches, from drystone walls to grassy meadows. For thousands

of years, such farmland habitats continued to support the growing population, while also sustaining a rich variety of wild things.

During the twentieth century, though, the production of food stepped up another gear. World War II (1939–45), especially, saw the start of a drive to maximize productivity, with an increasing reliance placed on home-grown produce during wartime. This impetus continued over the last century, with agribusiness emerging as a multi-billion-pound industry, backed up by advances in cutting-edge sciences as diverse as genetics, biochemisty and yield-mapping techniques. Inevitably, though, as new technologies were deployed to increase productivity, our farmland became ever more hostile to the wild things that it had once supported.

In the light of such developments, it's little wonder that the plants of our farmlands, such as burnt orchid (*Neotinea ustulata*) and prickly poppy (*Papaver argemone*), have experienced more change and, in some cases, more decline than species in any other habitat. Fortunately, some are tough and resilient enough to adapt to the harsh new environments imposed on them by modern agriculture, but many others are not.

Yet, awareness of these changes, with a corresponding shift in our own attitudes and a determination to remedy the situation means that all might not be lost …

OPPOSITE Sally collects bales of hay in Yorkshire, northern England. Hay, which is essentially dried grass, is fed to livestock during the winter.

BELOW Chris surveys a field of wheat in Kent, southeast England. As much as 1.9 million hectares of this cereal crop are grown each year in the British Isles.

CROP FIELDS

Each autumn or spring, more than 3 million hectares of cultivated fields in the British Isles are ploughed and tilled to produce a fine seed bed for crops such as wheat (*Triticum aestivum*), barley (*Hordeum vulgare*), oats (*Avena sativa*) or rape (*Brassica napus*). By late summer the ripe crop is harvested and in autumn or spring the age-old annual cycle of turning and tilling the soil is repeated.

Remarkably, though, the yearly turning of the soil doesn't merely prepare crop fields for sowing but also provides a habitat for a wide range of arable flowers, such as poppies. What, you might wonder, are poppies doing in cereal fields in the first place? Alongside the crop, they have evolved to complete their life cycle within one year, flowering and shedding their seed before dying. Only when the soil is turned again, exposing the seeds to light, which stimulates their germination, do the poppies appear once more. Like other arable species, they make the most of the opportunity provided by our cultivation and, when conditions are right, they pop up and grasp their chance to grow in huge numbers, producing vast quantities of seed for future generations.

Their very success, though, has created a conflict with our modern farming interests. With the need for ever-greater crop productivity, arable flowers are no longer welcome in our fields because they compete with crops for light, water and nutrients, reducing yields. The field flowers are only doing what's best for them but, unfortunately, it's to the detriment of crops. To eradicate arable flowers, crops are sprayed several times a year with highly effective herbicides, some of which have been developed to target individual species. Crops are also planted closely, reducing the space for other species to grow. After the crop seed is sown, fertilizers are spread to maximize its growth, creating rich soils that many arable plants cannot tolerate. Seed-cleaning technology has also been improved to ensure that crop seed is as pure as possible and to prevent arable flowers from spreading from field to field.

Despite such intensive measures, arable plants have evolved to tough it out and don't give up easily. Not all are susceptible to the herbicides and some have even developed a tolerance to them. Many have also evolved a biological trick that enables them to bounce back at the first opportunity, quite literally (see pp.201–3). In fact, a battle is being played out between farmers and plants in our arable fields today. We can watch the story unfold across our poppy fields.

BELOW The annual cycle of crop production begins with the plough, which turns the topsoil over, bringing buried nutrients to the surface.

OPPOSITE BOTTOM The combine harvester brings the annual cycle of crop production to an end, gathering the grain and leaving straw behind ready for baling.

MORE THAN JUST DAILY BREAD

Around the world, the human race is almost entirely dependent on grass – not as puzzling as you might think when you realize that the large grass family (*Poaceae*) includes our staple cereal crops, such as wheat, barley, oats, corn (*Zea mays*) and rice (*Oryza sativa*), which in turn provide our major sources of carbohydrates. As well as yielding grains for cereals, these crops provide flour for breads, pastas, noodles, cakes and biscuits, along with malt for brewing and distilling. As if that weren't enough, our primary sources of meat and milk, such as cattle and sheep, graze on various grasses, especially ryegrass (*Lolium perenne*) and bents (*Agrostis* sp.). Further afield, 80 per cent of our sugar comes from the tropical grass sugar cane (*Saccharum* sp.), the world's largest crop

yield, with 1.69 billion tonnes grown in 2010. At home, our farmed landscape is dominated by the cultivation of grasses (below). From cereal fields to grazed pastures, 14.2 million hectares of land are dedicated to all types of grasses, without which we'd not survive – something to chew on when you're next mowing the lawn.

ABOVE *A natural spectacle like no other, the blaze of red comes from a flush of common poppies growing in their thousands in a cultivated field untouched by herbicide.*

OPPOSITE *The spectacular decline in prickly poppy (inset) since 1987 is clear from a comparison of its paired distribution maps (bottom). It is now found in less than half of the 10km squares that it once occupied.*

POPPIES

When did you last see a field full of poppies? Although an iconic image of the British farming landscape and a much loved emblem of our fallen soldiers, the once familiar carpet of blood-red flowers in a sun-soaked sea of wheat or barley is no longer a common sight in our countryside. Not all poppies are the same, though, and some might be doing better than others. Five different types are found in arable fields: common poppy (*Papaver rhoeas*), opium poppy (*P. somniferum*), prickly poppy (*P. argemone*), rough poppy (*P. hybridum*) and the long-headed poppy (*P. dubium*). To see how poppies have fared on our farmlands, we'll look at three that illustrate how one has suffered, how another has toughed it out and how a third has even benefited from our agricultural activity.

A poppy of the cornfields

Of all our cornfield poppies, prickly poppies have suffered the biggest decline in the last fifty years as can be seen from their distribution maps (opposite), where they've disappeared from many areas completely. Highly susceptible to herbicides and unable to

FLOWERING TIMES

	J	F	M	A	M	J	J	A	S	O	N	D
Prickly poppy	✿	✿	✿	✿	✿	✿	✿	✿	✿	✿	✿	✿

grow among the competitive crops of the field or to tolerate the nitrogen-rich fertilizer spread on our crops, prickly poppy has become one of the top forty declining plants in the British Isles.

In some areas, such as Salisbury Plain in Wiltshire, southern England, prickly poppies can still be found. The best places to hunt for them now are the spots missed by the extended boom of the herbicide sprayer – most often in the corners of the fields and around the gateways. Usually, though, only a handful of surviving plants will be seen. Unfortunately, the same pattern of decline is repeated in the distribution maps for many of our arable plants (see pp.206–9). Other poppies, however, have had an easier time, such as common and opium poppies (see overleaf).

PRICKLY POPPY
PAPAVER ARGEMONE

UP TO 1987

TODAY

WARNING PLANT AT RISK WARNING

BELOW Like common poppy here, all poppies have just four petals. Their main flowering starts in June and July but they can continue blooming until October.

BOTTOM Chris inspects poppies in a sea of red on Salisbury Plain in Wiltshire, southern England.

A poppy to remember

Although common poppy is also extremely sensitive to herbicides, it is more widespread than prickly poppy, as it grows in a wider range of soil types. Where crop fields have been left unsprayed, the annual plants grow afresh from seed each year in huge numbers to colour our fields once again. Common poppy is actually even increasing in some areas (see opposite), but how can this be if farmers are using more and more herbicides on their fields? Several factors have probably encouraged common poppy's increase across the British Isles.

Agri-environment benefits

Government agri-environment schemes (AES) pay farmers to manage their land in a way that will benefit wildlife. One of the simplest and most effective changes in management is to leave arable fields unsprayed. Either the whole field is left untouched, or just the margins, the so-called conservation headlands. The results can be astonishing – within a year many arable plants quickly return and even rarities, such as pheasant's-eye (*Adonis annua*), start reappearing. If you see a strip of poppies along a field margin, it's likely to be the result of an AES.

COMMON POPPY
PAPAVER RHOEAS

1962

TODAY

New habitats
Poppies seem to be spreading into any areas where the soil has been disturbed, such as waste ground and rubbish tips, building sites and new roads. The prevalence of such sites might explain the plant's increase.

Wildflower seed mixes
Due to the increased use of wildflower seed mixes, more poppies are cropping up in parks and the wildflower areas of towns and cities as well as on roadsides and roundabouts.

Waking a sleeping beauty
How can poppies and other arable plants reappear so quickly after herbicide spraying has been stopped? The secret lies buried in the soil – literally, in the form of dormant seed. All arable plants are annuals, so their main aim in life is to live fast and die young, producing as much seed as possible in one short summer season. A single poppy might shed more than 60,000 seeds on to the surface of the soil as it dies. Because they live in fields that are regularly

Comparing the two plant maps for common poppy in 1962 and today, this species appears to have actually increased in the British Isles, especially in Wales, Ireland, northwest England and some parts of Scotland.

cultivated, the seed gets ploughed under the surface, where it lies dormant, a state in which it can remain viable for years – in fact, experiments have shown that the dormant seed of many arable plants can survive for decades and poppy seeds can remain alive but latent for more than eighty years. As a result, the soil of any arable field is absolutely packed full of dormant seed, which is why it's called the 'soil seed bank'. As long as some plants of a particular species get a chance to grow and shed their seed every few years, a fresh 'deposit' can be made into the seed bank, increasing the likelihood of that species' reappearance in the field for years to come.

What conditions are needed to encourage the buried seed to germinate? In many cases, it's incredibly simple – just a brief flash of light is all it takes to waken the sleeping seed. Whenever a seed is brought back to the surface by the plough, its dark slumber is broken by a glimmer of light, which instantly sets off a chemical signal prompting the seed to start germinating. Awakened by light, the seed 'knows' that it's back on the surface again and its opportunity has come to grow and flower, which it will do, just so long as it isn't doused with herbicide along the way.

If you thought that eighty years was a long time to remain dormant, that's nothing. Frozen seeds of narrow-leaved campion

(*Silene stenophylla*), which has lain stored in the burrows of arctic ground squirrels in Siberia, have been brought back to life in the laboratory – and they were a mere 32,000 years old.

A symbol of the fallen

The existence of the soil seed bank helps explain why our common poppy has become a symbol of remembrance. The opening lines of the poem 'In Flanders Fields' written by John McCrae in 1915 describe the poppies that sprang up on the freshly dug graves of fallen soldiers during World War I (1914–18):

> *In Flanders fields the poppies blow*
> *Between the crosses, row on row,*
> *That mark our place; and in the sky*
> *The larks, still bravely singing, fly*
> *Scarce heard amid the guns below.*

Released from their slumber, poppies grew in abundance on the churned-up soil of battlefields. Through the popularity of the poem, blood-red poppies were adopted as a symbol of remembrance by the Royal British Legion in 1921, and have been worn ever since on Poppy Day.

In medieval times, poppies were called corn-roses, reflecting their rosy colour and field habitat. In traditional folklore, picking the beautiful flower was thought to provoke summer storms, which led to the poppy's other old names, thundercups and lightnings.

A controversial poppy

Not all our poppies are regarded as weeds to be removed from crop fields. Opium poppy (*P. somniferum*) has been cultivated for thousands of years and is sometimes grown as a crop in its own right, mainly for its sedative effects (see opposite). The map of its distribution (below) tells a very different story from that of prickly poppy. Having now reached almost all lowland areas except the western and northern coast of Scotland, it's ranked among the country's top forty fastest-spreading plants.

Opium poppy has a very long history in the British Isles, having been introduced from the eastern Mediterranean region for its culinary and medicinal properties in the Bronze Age, *c*.2500–800 BC (see p.210). Indeed, its Latin name *somniferum* (sleep-bringing) refers to the sedative effects of the opiates contained in its sap. The plant is also widely grown in gardens, as it's a very beautiful flower that comes in a variety of colours and forms, including ruffled and double petals.

The popularity of opium poppy in gardens partly explains its remarkable spread across the British Isles since 1962 (below). Another

The distribution maps for opium poppy show its remarkable spread across the British Isles since 1962. It has increased fourfold in the last fifty years.

OPIUM POPPY
PAPAVER SOMNIFERUM

1962

TODAY

TEARS OF THE POPPY

Opium poppy has been cultivated in western Asia since *c.*4000 BC for the sedative and analgesic properties of its milky white sap (latex). Today it is still harvested, whether for medicinal morphine or narcotic cocaine and heroin. Australia, Turkey and India are the major suppliers of morphine, while Afghanistan produces 82 per cent of the world's illegal opium. The drug is harvested from the poppy's 'tears' – a milky white latex, which coagulates on exposure to air, sealing the poppy's wounds. Poppy latex is collected by scoring ripening seed pods with shallow cuts. The sap that pours out to seal the plant's cuts dries to a sticky brown resin, which contains up to 92 per cent of morphine and related chemicals.

reason probably relates to the nature of its preferred habitat: unlike common and prickly poppies, opium poppy does not naturally appear in crop fields, so has not suffered the decline that's hit other poppies (see pp.198–203). In the wild, it's generally a plant of disturbed soil, flourishing on roadsides, roundabouts, waste ground, building sites and rubbish tips. Its astonishing spread in the last fifty years is probably down to the fact that soil is increasingly disturbed and moved around today, with new developments, road-building, urban sprawl and edge-of-town building sites now common. The poppy's recent increase might also reflect climate change – our milder winters are more comfortable for a plant that originally came from the Mediterranean.

Opium poppy is, however, now being grown on a new scale, which might soon swell its numbers. Faced by a global shortage of medicinal morphine, pharmaceutical companies in the West have developed poppy strains capable of yielding comparable levels of opiates to those achieved in the warmer climates of the poppy's traditional growing grounds in Asia. For the last ten years, in fact, fields of opium poppies have been grown in southern England and reaped mechanically by combine harvesters. In full flower, they're a spectacular sight, which we could be seeing more of in the future.

Opium poppy flowers are very distinctive, usually pale lilac with a darker blotch at the base of the petals. Garden forms come in a wide range of colours, including reds, pinks and purples.

CORNFIELD CASUALTIES

The arable flowers that traditionally grew in our crop fields, adding characteristic colour and variety to the British landscape, have been decreasing over the last half century. To give a rough idea of the scale of decline, let's look at what's at the top of the list of disappearing species, what's on the edge of extinction and what's already been lost. Brace yourselves, it's not a happy tale.

In decline

Looking at the distribution maps (see pp.34, 207), we can work out which plants have undergone the biggest decline in the British Isles over the last fifty years. Incredibly, nine of the top ten disappearing species are arable. Of the top thirty declining plants, twenty are cornfield flowers, among them the following:

Pheasant's-eye
(*Adonis annua*)
Night-flowering catchfly
(*Silene noctiflora*)
Spreading hedge-parsley
(*Torilis arvensis*)
Small-flowered catchfly
(*Silene gallica*)
Broad-fruited cornsalad
(*Valerianella rimosa*)

WARNING PLANT AT RISK WARNING

RIGHT *Wildflowers in decline, from top to bottom: pheasant's-eye, night-flowering catchfly, spreading hedge-parsley, small-flowered catchfly and broad-fruited cornsalad.*

OPPOSITE *Wildflowers on the edge, from top to bottom: upright goosefoot, red hemp-nettle, shepherd's-needle and corn cleavers, whose distribution map (bottom) illustrates the dramatic decline in this once widespread cornfield plant, now known to exist from just one site.*

On the edge

A plant that is under the highest level of threat is formally classified as Critically Endangered, which means that it's on the very edge of extinction. Once again, arable plants seem to be the most vulnerable, as the majority of Critically Endangered species currently grow in cultivated fields. The worst affected include:

Upright goosefoot (*Chenopodium urbicum*)
Red hemp-nettle (*Galeopsis angustifolia*)
Shepherd's-needle (*Scandix pecten-veneris*)
Corn cleavers (*Galium tricornutum*)
Thorow-wax (*Bupleurum rotundifolium*)
Darnel (*Lolium temulentum*)
Corn buttercup (*Ranunculus arvensis*)

CORN CLEAVERS
GALIUM TRICORNUTUM

UP TO 2000

TODAY

WARNING
PLANT AT RISK
WARNING

Truly extinct

It takes a lot for a plant to be declared completely extinct in the British Isles. Not only must every last individual plant disappear but, just in case it pops up again somewhere, a further twenty-five years should elapse without the species being recorded in the wild before it can be deemed truly extinct. Just twenty species of flowering plants have been declared extinct in the British Isles. Of these, six grew in cultivated fields, more than in any other single habitat. In order of their disappearance, they are:

1955 Narrow-leaved cudweed
   (*Filago gallica*)
1962 Small bur-parsley
   (*Caucalis platycarpos*)
1969 Violet horned-poppy
   (*Papaver bivalve* subsp. *hybridum*)
1971 Lamb's succory
   (*Arnoseris minima*)
1972 Interrupted brome
   (*Bromus interruptus*)
1975 Downy hemp-nettle
   (*Galeopsis segetum*)

Some of these, such as narrow-leaved cudweed and interrupted brome, have since been reintroduced to places where they once grew, but the truly wild populations have now disappeared.

It's hard to hear the harsh facts, but they paint the true picture of our arable fields today. It's a pattern of loss, with large swathes of our countryside now devoid of many of their characteristic plants and flowers.

Toughing it out

Not all arable plants have suffered quite the same fate, though. On the bright side, the toughest and most tolerant still survive – the ones that can compete with the crops, shrug off the effects of some herbicide, and benefit from all that fertilizer. Walk into any intensively farmed arable field and you're likely to find a handful of ten or twenty survivors, including some familiar flowers:

Field pansy (*Viola arvensis*)
Sun spurge (*Euphorbia helioscopia*)
Common fumitory (*Fumaria officinalis*)
Common chickweed (*Stellaria media*)
Cleavers (*Galium aparine*)

But it's a very short list compared with the 160 or more cornfield flowers that have been recorded growing in British crop fields over the past fifty years.

OPPOSITE Truly extinct wildflowers, from top to bottom: narrow-leaved cudweed, violet horned-poppy, lamb's succory, interrupted brome and downy hemp-nettle.

LEFT AND BELOW Cornfield flowers toughing it out, from top to bottom: field pansy, sun spurge, common fumitory, common chickweed and cleavers (below).

Living archaeology

Many arable plants, such as cornflower (*Centaurea cyanus*), are not actually native to the British Isles but were brought here by early farmers a very long time ago. Known as the archaeophytes – literally, 'ancient plants' – they form a very special group.

Digging up the past

Around 10,000 years ago, agriculture first developed on the Fertile Crescent in southwest Asia and gradually spread across northwestern Europe, reaching the British Isles in about 5,500 BC. Migrating farmers brought a variety of recently developed crops to cultivate in their new fields. Wheat, barley and oats were commonly grown, along with other crops such as flax (*Linum usitatissimum*) for oil and fibre. Systems of bartering were still common, so, rather than exchanging money for goods, farmers swapped bags of crop seeds, which also contained the seeds of arable plants.

Evidence from archaeological digs, such as the presence of seeds in grain storage pits and middens (domestic waste heaps), gives

Some of our most ancient flowers that arrived in the British Isles from between 4,500 and 1,900 years ago; cornflower (above right), corn marigold (below) and opium poppy (below right).

us a good idea of when different species arrived in the British Isles. Shepherd's purse, for instance, first appeared during the Stone Age, *c.*4000–2500 BC; corn marigolds, prickly and opium poppies arrived during the Bronze Age, *c.*2500–800 BC; cornflowers and common poppies during the Iron Age, *c.*800 BC–AD 100; and corn buttercups with the Romans, *c.*54 BC–AD 410.

As archaeophytes have been so closely associated with our culture and farming practices for more than 7,500 years, they have immense cultural and historical significance. They are, quite literally, a direct link to our ancient history – a living archaeology, providing a record of our past activities on the land. In the light of these associations, we treat archaeophytes as we would our native species, affording them conservation status and including them in our efforts to restore threatened plants to the countryside. When you next see a field full of poppies, remember the Iron Age farmers who first brought them here.

GRASSLANDS AND MEADOWS

Much of our countryside still looks like a rural idyll, despite modern developments and transport networks crisscrossing the landscape (see chapter 3). Rolling hills, burgeoning hedgerows and dense woodlands outline the patchwork of lush green fields – it's a pastoral picture that typifies the British landscape in the popular imagination. Look a bit closer, though, and you might see that something is missing from our green and pleasant land …

PASTURES GREEN

It's true that our islands are still green. There are 12.4 million hectares of grassland in the British Isles, which is 68 per cent of the country's total area of farmland. Just as with arable crops, though, there has been a massive increase in the demand for what we produce from our green grasslands – milk, lamb and beef, for example. As a result, pastures are ploughed up and re-sown, often with a single strain of highly productive ryegrass (*Lolium perenne*). The fields are sprayed with herbicide to remove all other flowering plants and heavily fertilized to maximize growth, while any wet

BELOW Perennial ryegrass has been sown in pastures since the seventeenth century and is now one of our most widespread grasses.

BOTTOM Intensively farmed pastures are a distinctive billiard-table green and lack the diversity of flowering plants seen in flower meadows.

pastures are drained. The resulting billiard-table green fields are often cut twice a year to make silage (stored fodder). As a result of this agricultural 'improvement', it is estimated that 97 per cent of our flower-rich lowland meadows have been lost since 1940. Our land might still be green, but it's not quite as pleasant – certainly not as flower-rich, colourful or scented – as it once was.

WILDFLOWER MEADOWS

Some ancient grasslands, however, remain rich in wildflowers and other wild things. True meadows have escaped agricultural improvement and instead developed over decades or even centuries to become astonishing tapestries of life.

In the richest meadows, more than forty species of flowering plants can grow within a single square metre. The diverse growth seen in meadows doesn't mean that they're not carefully managed. Quite the opposite, in fact, for without an annual hay-cut in high summer, or heavy grazing by livestock from late summer to winter, the grass would grow long; shrubs, such as hawthorn and

OPPOSITE TOP A silver-washed fritillary searches for nectar in a flower meadow.

BELOW Trevor examines a flower-rich hay meadow in Muker, Swaledale, Yorkshire, awash with buttercups (Ranunculus acris), red clover (Trifolium pratense), white-flowered pignut (Conopodium majus) and pink spikes of common sorrel (Rumex acetosa).

blackthorn, would quickly become established; and wildflowers would disappear. Good meadows depend on good management.

The best meadows are almost like cities: they're bustling, never-ending hives of activity, twenty-four hours a day, 365 days a year. During the day, bees, butterflies and hoverflies are on the go, patrolling their patches for pollen and nectar. Plants soak up the sun's energy to grow and spread, shouldering aside their rivals to claim their neighbourhood; hares court and box their competitors; sparrow-hawks hover on the lookout for prey.

During the night, another hidden shift comes on watch. Moths seek out sweetly scented orchids, beetles scavenge, voles scuttle along their runs and barn owls sweep overhead, silently watching everything. Underground, a network of white fungal mycelium (mesh of filaments) decomposes decaying vegetation, while the roots of some plants penetrate those of their neighbours to steal their water and nutrients.

BELOW Ancient wildflower hay meadows provide a rich source of food plants, nectar and pollen. Bees, butterflies and bugs all find a home in the meadows, which in turn support other insects, birds and mammals.

COMMON MEADOW FLOWERS

Our flower meadows can offer a many-coloured richness and a wide variety of wildflowers. Here are some of the more common species that you should be able to spot in any ancient wildflower meadow.

	Yellow rattle (*Rhinanthus minor*)	The roots of this plant tap into those of the grasses around it, stealing their nutrients. When its seeds are ripe, they rattle in their pods – a sign to the farmer that the meadow's grass is ready to cut and dry for making hay.
	Oxeye daisy (*Leucanthemum vulgare*)	Like all daisies, the apparent flowers of this plant are actually disks made up of hundreds of tiny individual flowers (florets), each with a valuable dose of nectar. The plant's large white flowers are also known as moon daisies.
	Common spotted orchid (*Dactylorhiza fuchsii*)	One of our most common orchids, it's easily recognizable by its pinkish-lilac flowers, which appear in dense spikes above spotted leaves. Each flower has a landing platform for pollinating bees and a short tube with a reward of nectar.
	Sweet vernal-grass (*Anthoxanthum odoratum*)	When dry, this is the plant that gives hay its characteristic sweet, slightly vanilla smell, due to the presence of two chemicals, courmarin and benzoic acid. Courmarin has been in the production of perfume since 1882.
	Common bird's-foot-trefoil (*Lotus corniculatus*)	The leaves are a valuable food source for the caterpillars of six-spot burnet moths and common blue butterflies. The plant's name reflects the shape of its seedpods and leaves, but it's also called bacon-and-eggs after the colour of its flowers.
	Wood crane's-bill (*Geranium sylvaticum*)	Characteristic of northern hay meadows, the flowers of this geranium produce a blue-grey dye that was used by the Norsemen of ancient Europe to dye their war cloaks, believing that it would protect soldiers in battle.
	Yorkshire fog (*Holcus lanatus*)	From a distance the slightly pinkish flower spikes of this soft, downy grass can look like mist settled on a meadow, hence the flower's common name. Yorkshire fog leaves are eaten by the caterpillars of small skipper butterflies.
	Eyebright (*Euphrasia* spp.)	An indicator plant of ancient meadows, eighteen different species of eyebright grow in the British Isles. The tiny white flowers have a purple stain, which led to the traditional belief that eyebright could cure eye conditions.

Meadow orchids

For many people, coming across a flower-rich meadow during a walk in the country offers the perfect opportunity to hunt for orchids. A large variety grow naturally in grasslands, but the decline of several, such as frog orchid (*Coeloglossum viride*), lesser butterfly orchid (*Platanthera bifolia*) and green-winged orchid (*Orchis morio*), stems from the conversion of old pastures into agriculturally improved grasslands. None better illustrates the decline of meadow flowers than burnt orchid (*Neotinea ustulata*).

Found almost exclusively in chalk and limestone meadows that have been grazed short by sheep and cattle, burnt orchid has declined spectacularly in the last fifty years – in fact, in 60 per cent of the counties where it once grew, such as Norfolk, Devon and Shropshire, it is now extinct. Only on Salisbury Plain in Wiltshire, southern England, is it still found in quantity, growing on the warm sunny slopes of ancient Iron Age earthworks that have been protected from plough, herbicide and fertilizer.

ABOVE AND BELOW
Since the year 2000, burnt orchid (above) has only been found in thirty-seven 10km squares, having disappeared from 86 per cent of the hectads where it once grew (below).

BURNT ORCHID
NEOTINEA USTULATA

UP TO 2000

TODAY

WARNING PLANT AT RISK WARNING

FARMLANDS

How to age a meadow

A remarkable but little-known biological clock allows us to estimate the age of a wildflower meadow. It helps to have an eye for buttercups.

What you need
1 × ancient wildflower meadow
1 × sunny day
1 × notebook and pen
1 × calculator
1 × dog needing a good walk

Two or three species of buttercup often grow together in flower-rich meadows (above right).

WHICH BUTTERCUP IS WHICH?			
Name	Bulbous buttercup (*R. bulbosus*)	Creeping buttercup (*R. repens*)	Meadow buttercup (*R. acris*)
Sepals (the small green bits under the petals)	Reflexed backwards against the flower stem	Not reflexed backwards, the sepals lie against the petal	Not reflexed backwards, the sepals lie against the petal
Stems	All upright	Some creep over the surface of the ground	All upright
Leaves	Finely cut with pointed tips	Deeply lobed with rounded tips	Finely cut with pointed tips

The method

Once you have gained the permission of the meadow's landowner, take your dog for a good long walk around the field. Every few minutes, glance at the flowers around you and try to find the closest creeping buttercup (*R. repens*). Just look at the table opposite to see how. Now try to pick out a single creeping buttercup by eye. Then look at it more closely and count the number of petals. Most creeping buttercups have five petals, but every now and again you'll find one with six, or sometimes even seven or eight petals. Note down in a tally whether your flower has five petals or more than five. Move on, then stop again after a few paces and repeat the exercise. Try not to look for buttercups with more than five petals – just pick up the flower that you spot first. Once you have counted 100 buttercups, stop and count up the number with more than five petals; then multiply this number by seven. The result is the approximate age of your meadow in years.

THE SCIENCE

Creeping buttercup does much of its reproduction by 'creeping around' – quite literally, as most of the buttercup's new plants grow from its side shoots; as these spread, the older bits of the plant die off, leaving fragments (called ramets) to disperse, or 'creep off' around the meadow. The entire creeping buttercup population in a meadow might actually originate from just a few original starter plants, which over the years fragment and increase in number, spreading around the meadow.

In time, each fragment becomes an older version of the original plant, but still carries identical genes to its parent. With age, some of the genes start to mutate and produce flowers with an extra petal or two. As the fragments continue to age, more and more mutate and generate flowers with extra petals. This mutation happens at a rate of about one plant in every seven years, hence we can age a meadow by the number of flowers with extra petals.

A creeping buttercup might therefore stem from the fragment of an original starter buttercup that first grew when the meadow originated, quite possibly one or two centuries ago.

If the meadow is ploughed up, though, all the surviving fragments will be buried and die but that won't be the end of the story, as new plants will start up again from dormant seed left in the soil. At this starter stage, the buttercup's remarkable biological clock is reset. At first no mutations will occur until, approximately seven years later, a six-petalled buttercup will appear again.

A creeping buttercup flower, whose ageing genes have mutated to produce an extra petal (top). Flowers with between seven and twelve petals are not uncommon and sometimes they are packed with extra petals (above), such as this fully-double type (var. pleniflorus).

FARM LICHENS AND MOSSES

Sometimes it's the small things that react to the big changes … The landscape of the British Isles has altered dramatically because of agriculture, which has affected many tiny creatures, including lichens and mosses.

Ideal homes on the farm

Once people had started farming the land, around 8,000 years ago, they created an array of habitats for wild things, such as hedges and ditches, walls and fences. Mosses and lichens found a wide variety of places in which to live within the cracks and crevices

Anaptychia ciliaris (bottom), *also known as eagle's claw lichen, grows on nutrient-enriched wayside trees, while a multitude of mosses and lichens flourish in the crevices of ancient boundary walls (below).*

of these wonderful new habitats, ranging from drystone walls to tree-lined avenues. Some lichens, such as *Anaptychia ciliaris,* became adapted to the nutrient-enriched bark of wayside trees that grew along the edge of fields, and enjoyed the nutrient-enriched dust deposited on the bark from cattle dung and the dust stirred up by their hooves.

Other lichens, such as *Cyphelium inquinans*, which live on dead trees, had previously been confined to the dead trees in the Caledonian pinewoods of Scotland. With the growth of farming, however, they were able to colonize the dead wood used to make farm fences, and spread throughout the whole country as a result.

Some clever mosses, such as bird's claw beard-moss (*Barbula unguiculata*), adapted to the open ground of crop fields, where

have been developed that can be sown over winter. Although these changes may have only a small effect at a local level – the odd hedgerow taken out here, the odd tree felled over there – when we look at the national picture, they're having a huge impact on the future of the tiny creatures on the farm. As arable habitats are lost, so are the homes of the mosses and lichens. It starts with the small things, but eventually the birds and the badgers will notice too.

The original sites of Cyphelium inquinans *(inset square, below right) in the Caledonian pinewoods (right), from where this lichen has now spread to fence posts countrywide (above).*

there would be little competition from other plants among the bare soil after harvest. To synchronize with the cycles of field crops, many such mosses developed a super-fast, short-lived life-cycle, enabling them to reproduce and move on before the next crop was planted during the following spring.

Small change, big difference

Unfortunately today, as our population has grown, we have begun to farm more intensively and many of our traditional arable habitats have been lost. Hedgerows and wayside trees, for instance, have been removed to make way for bigger fields; drystone walls and wooden fences are often replaced with wire-stock netting; and fields are no longer left as stubble during the winter, as new crop varieties

LOOKING TO THE FUTURE

The scale of the loss of once familiar flowers across our farmlands over the last fifty years has been laid bare by the latest distribution maps, which clearly highlight the significant effect that modern farming has had on our countryside. The consequences have been dramatic for all our wild things, which have been steadily pushed out of their traditional homes by intensive, specialized agriculture. Though the damaging effects might start with plants, they soon have a knock-on effect on all the wild things that they sustain.

Fortunately, we've now begun to appreciate the full cost of the drive for high yields and productivity in modern agriculture. As we witness a loss of colour and wildflowers across our farmlands, we're increasingly reminded that a countryside rich in a wide variety of plants, birds, bugs and animals brings many benefits to farming. Flower-rich grasslands, for example, improve the health of our grazing livestock and the quality of the meat that they produce, as well as supporting a myriad of pollinating insects – everything is interconnected in a complex web of life.

Flourishing together, wild common poppies and a crop of oilseed rape flower in September on the Dorset Downs, southwest England.

Today, the first steps are being taken to develop a more balanced farming environment for the future. Many farmers, encouraged by agri-environment schemes and other incentives, are now working hard, often in partnership with conservation organizations, to encourage wildlife back on to their farms (see p.200). The success of these schemes has shown that profitable farming and caring for all our plants and animals can go hand in hand. To achieve the best results all round, farmers and conservationists are increasingly adopting a collaborative approach to problems, with the distribution maps providing an invaluable resource that informs their dialogue. Even so, we should never expect to return to some remembered pastoral idyll. Although we can't turn the clock back – our farmland today is a very different place compared with what it was fifty years ago – we can work for new productive solutions.

While the first steps towards richer, more diverse farmlands have already been taken, much more needs to be done on a far bigger scale. Only then will we begin to see the signs of recovery and colour returning to our countryside.

CHAPTER SEVEN
BACK TO
THE FUTURE

PREVIOUS PAGE Cushions of sea thrift (Armeria maritima) grow on the clifftops near Porthcothan Bay, Cornwall, southwest England. How much will this view have changed in fifty years' time?

Thanks to the work of thousands of dedicated BSBI volunteer plant detectives, who've been gathering evidence over the past fifty years, we can now look back and see the changes that have taken place in our landscape (see pp.24–8). In this short period, less than one lifetime, our villages, cities and countryside have altered as never before.

The patchwork of small hay fields and grazing pastures that characterize the Yorkshire Dales, northern England, are a rare sight in our modern farmed landscape.

We've carved out lines in the landscape with our network of roads and railways, connecting cities and houses across the country; we've released myriad exotic plants into the wild; we've converted our traditional patchwork of species-rich cornfields and meadows into deserts dominated by sterile crops and pastures, while many of our native woodlands have fallen into disrepair; and we've altered the very composition of the soil, water and air with herbicides, fertilizers and emissions.

The wild things living and growing alongside us have responded in quite different ways to the enormous upheavals that we've imposed on their habitats. Some, such as Danish scurvygrass, have flourished, moving into new places and making the most of fresh opportunities (see pp.92–104); others, such as corn buttercup and burnt orchid, have suffered, disappearing from our meadows, woodlands, fields and hedgerows in a gradual loss of colour that often goes unnoticed (see pp.198–209).

Our wild things will no doubt face yet more changes in the next fifty years and they will continue to respond, whether by adapting and thriving or by declining. But now, for the first time ever, armed with evidence gleaned from the distribution maps, we can begin to grasp the magnitude of past shifts in the environment, to spot emerging trends and maybe even to predict what future developments might lie in store.

THE DRIVERS OF CHANGE

Looking at the national maps for particular species is quite fascinating, as each one illustrates an individual story of struggle and success or, sometimes, of failure. However, it's only when the maps for all species growing in the wild are drawn together and compared that we have an invaluable system of analysis at our disposal. Reviewing the latest *Atlas of the British and Irish Flora* as a whole enables us to see the bigger picture and the large-scale trends taking place in the British Isles today. By looking behind these wider patterns, we can start to understand what's driving the changes that we're seeing. Five key factors emerge:

 Fertilizer rain

The atmospheric nitrogen released into the air from car exhausts, industry and agriculture is deposited across our countryside as 'fertilizer rain'. Soaking into the ground, nitrogen deposits cause high levels of nutrients in the soil, especially in areas of intense rainfall, where up to 24kg of nitrogen per hectare can fall each year. While some plants thrive on this fertilizer, other species prefer nutrient-poor soils. Inevitably, the ones that do well on nitrogen – usually the aggressive, weedy plants, such as nettles and cleavers – are now out-competing smaller, more delicate plants, such as harebell (*Campanula rotundifolia*) and lady's bedstraw (*Galium verum*).

Harebell is a poor competitor and cannot stand up to more aggressive species, such as coarse grasses, which thrive on the nitrogen that is deposited as fertilizer rain. As a result, harebell is beginning to decline in some areas.

Loss of traditional habitats

As we saw in chapter 6, the demands of agricultural production have turned species-rich meadows, wetlands and grasslands into species-poor fields dominated by single crops, such as wheat or ryegrass. As our ancient grasslands are ploughed up and re-seeded, as our wetlands are drained and as cleaner crops are grown, the diversity of our farmland habitats has declined (see chapter 6).

Fewer small, mixed farms

Until the mid twentieth century, many farms were mixed, combining the rearing of livestock with the cultivation of cereals. Each farm maintained some grassy pastures for grazing livestock along with a few crop fields for growing a variety of cereals, including oats, barley and wheat. Both the fields and the crops would be rotated over the years – a diversity of management that led to a diversity of species. Today, though, intensive and specialized farming practices have limited diversity and rotation. Modern farms tend to concentrate on either livestock or crops. In the north and west, for example, there's a trend for farms to be predominantly devoted to livestock, while those in the south and east are mostly arable. Such specialization leads to a uniformity of landscape with little room for species that might need different habitats. As a result, plant diversity has declined.

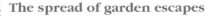

The spread of garden escapes

As we saw in chapter 5, the escape and spread of non-native species from our gardens has significantly changed the character of our towns, cities and countryside. While many escaped species, such as pineappleweed, are benign and add colour and interest to several habitats, invasive species, such as rhododendron, Spanish bluebell and New Zealand pigmyweed, all have the potential to upset the delicate balance of nature (see pp.57–71, 159–71, 182–6).

A shift in climate

As we're now experiencing hotter and longer growing seasons and milder, wetter winters, it's become apparent that plants are responding to the warmer weather, not only by growing or flowering earlier in the year but also by appearing in new parts of the British Isles. Warmth-loving plants, such as hart's-tongue fern, mossy stonecrop and bee orchid (*Ophrys apifera*), are now spreading north and west (see pp.48–9, 79–80).

FAR LEFT Rhododendron has increased greatly in the last fifty years.

CENTRE LEFT Spanish bluebell, which is spreading to many new areas, now threatens native bluebells.

ABOVE LEFT The white flowers of invasive Japanese knotweed are an all too familiar sight in the British Isles today.

BELOW LEFT A parched river bed was an unusual sight in our rainy country until extreme weather became more frequent. During the drought of 2006, several rivers dried up, such as the River Skirfare in Littondale, Yorkshire, northern England.

BELOW One of the plants responding to climate change, the warmth-loving bee orchid, is now venturing further north and west as the weather heats up.

NATURE'S LOTTERY

What can we learn from the patterns of the past? What do the stories of individual plants tell us? Looking at the national distribution maps as a whole, what clearly emerges is that some species seem to be natural winners, while others have succumbed to the changes wrought by our modern farming practices and lifestyles, by invading garden escapes and by climate change.

The winners

The five plants that have increased the most in the last fifty years are:

Yellow loosestrife (*Lysimachia punctata*)
Buddleja (*Buddleia davidii*)
Cherry laurel (*Prunus laurocerasus*)
American willowherb (*Epilobium ciliatum*)
Purple toadflax (*Linaria purpurea*)

All five are garden escapes and most are invasive (see chapter 5). Their stories indicate that similar non-native species are likely to increase in the future, perhaps with an impact on our native plants.

PLANT AT RISK WARNING

The losers

The five plants that have decreased the most in the past fifty years are:

Thorow-wax (*Bupleurum rotundifolium*)
Corn buttercup (*Ranunculus arvensis*)
Corn cleavers (*Galium tricornutum*)
Upright goosefoot (*Chenopodium urbicum*)
Darnel (*Lolium temulentum*)

All but upright goosefoot grow in crop fields, warning us that this habitat is under extreme pressure. We need to pay special attention to our arable flowers to ensure that none become extinct in the next fifty years.

The winners (opposite), clockwise: yellow loosestrife, buddleja and cherry laurel; and the losers (left), from top to bottom: thorow-wax, corn buttercup and corn cleavers.

OPPOSITE With their rich tapestry of habitats, the warm coastal cliffs of southern England are especially important for plants. They're home to many rare native species, as well as new arrivals from abroad.

BELOW The surprising appearance on a Cornish cliff of some small-flowered tongue-orchids – usually more at home in the Mediterranean – provides evidence of our warming climate.

The next fifty years?

Making predictions about future change is fraught with difficulty, as we simply don't know exactly what changes will take place or how different species will respond. The only thing that we can be certain about is that in fifty years' time our landscape *will* have changed.

The main driving forces already discussed are likely to continue to exert an influence in the future. The effects of climate change, in particular, will become more apparent when plant populations respond, since they take longer than animals to react and move around; when they do, it's a sign that things really have changed. As the weather warms up, new species might well arrive on our shores – in fact, we've already seen the appearance of the distinctly Mediterranean small-flowered tongue-orchid (*Serapias parviflora*) in Cornwall. Its seeds, carried on the wind from France, have now found conditions here warm enough to stay.

It's certain that more non-native plants will spread from our gardens. Newly escaped species are being recorded all the time and weedy ones that like disturbed soil are likely to do especially well in the future, again encouraged by our warmer climate. Others, such as giant rhubarb and tree-of-heaven, are already potential new ecosystem engineers, posing yet more threats to native plants (see chapter 5).

Despite the continued disruption to plant habitats imposed by climate change and our modern lifestyle and farming practices, we're now at least alert to the loss of species and are particularly careful to pre-empt extinctions. Our rarest and most threatened plants receive special attention. Careful monitoring and recording is in place and a raft of conservation measures, such as reinstating coppicing and hay-cutting, can be used to help save our rarities before they reach the brink of extinction (see pp.235–6). For plants that are already on the edge, we can resort to reintroduction programmes, as in the case of lady's-slipper orchid (*Cypripedium calceolus*), a modern success story (see overleaf).

BELOW The pouch-shaped yellow lip of lady's-slipper orchid attracts small Andrena bees, which fall inside, then pollinate the flower when clambering out.

LADY'S-SLIPPER ORCHID

On a remote hillside in Yorkshire, a single plant grows. It's the last of its kind. Lady's-slipper orchid was once found in twenty-one of the country's 10km squares, mostly in the north of England from Derbyshire to Yorkshire, Cumbria and County Durham. Here it grew on steep slopes of wildflower-rich limestone grassland sheltered by open woodland.

It's without doubt our most flamboyant native orchid. Sporting an inflated chrome-yellow pouch and twisting burgundy petals, it looks as though it should be growing in the tropics rather than in the temperate British Isles, but the plant has paid a very heavy price for its good looks. During the eighteenth century, bunches of lady's-slipper orchids were supplied to local hotels and traded in markets for just 2s and 6d (12½p). Even worse, whole clumps were dug up from the wild and sold for people to grow in their gardens. The result was catastrophic – in 1917, lady's-slipper orchid was declared extinct in the British Isles.

LADY'S-SLIPPER ORCHID
CYPRIPEDIUM CALCEOLUS

UP TO 1917

TODAY

WARNING PLANT AT RISK WARNING

Then, quite by chance, in 1930, a single, last surviving plant was found on a wooded hillside in Yorkshire. Ever since, the existence of this orchid has been kept a closely guarded secret, protected by a small group of guardians, called the Cypripedium Committee. To prevent theft, the site of the orchid's reappearance is placed under twenty-four-hour surveillance during the plant's flowering period; and, occasionally, trip wires and CCTV have even been employed.

Orchid rescue mission

With just one native plant left in the wild, it was time for a rescue mission to bring this magnificent orchid back from the brink of extinction. A reintroduction programme was established by tracking down some of the orchids that had previously been taken from the wild to grow in gardens. When found, the garden orchids were used to cross-pollinate the single remaining wild plant

ABOVE After a wait of thirty years, Trevor fulfils a lifetime's ambition when he witnesses lady's-slipper orchid growing in the wild in the Yorkshire Dales, northern England.

OPPOSITE BOTTOM Lady's-slipper orchid once grew in many sites across northern England. The ongoing reintroduction programme aims eventually to restore plants to all their former sites. Today, two of these sites, as shown on the map, are now open to the public (opposite right).

FLOWERING TIMES														
		J	F	M	A	M	J	J	A	S	O	N	D	
Lady's-slipper orchid		❀	❀	❀	❀	❀	❀	❀	❀	❀	❀	❀	❀	

Rabbits, introduced to the British Isles by the Romans c.2000 years ago, are one of the main threats to young lady's-slipper orchid plants. To prevent rabbits nibbling the orchid's precious shoots, they're protected by sturdy wire cages.

growing in Yorkshire. The resulting seedlings are grown by a small group of dedicated and expert gardeners until they're big and strong enough to be planted back in the wild.

Since this reintroduction programme began in 1989, the number of sites with flowering plants has risen from one to eight. The main threats to the plant's survival are slugs and rabbits, which are being deterred by copper rings, slug pellets and cages. Alarmingly, people, too, remain a problem – in 2004 one of the best plants was attacked with a spade and half of it was dug up.

Thanks to the reintroduction programme, lady's-slipper orchids are beginning to flower in the wild again. In 2008, the plant's first seed-pod was produced after being fertilized by the small *Andrena* bees that pollinate its flowers. This rare beauty is not out of the woods yet, though. True success will only come when these seeds grow into plants that flower without our direct intervention, spreading by themselves through the hillsides where they once flourished. Only then will we really have undone the damage that we did in the past by uprooting wild orchids from their natural habitat.

In the meantime, as these orchids grow and mature, more and more flowers are produced – remarkably, in 2011, 127 flowers opened their petals. The success of the programme means that we can now see lady's-slipper orchid in the wild once more. Two sites, Gait Barrows Natural Nature Reserve in Lancashire and Kilnsey Park in Yorkshire, are now open to the public and attract thousands of visitors each year in early June. The sight of the flowers in the wild is breathtaking.

LESS COTTON WOOL, MORE BULLDOZERS

Conservation itself is constantly evolving as we learn more about the dynamic flux of nature. In the past, rare plants were often fenced off from the wild and left untouched, protected by a cage or a barbed-wire enclosure. Such defensive tactics, however, only served to isolate species from the very management on which they depended for their survival and, after a few years, these 'protected' species would disappear. We now appreciate that conservation is not about wrapping plants up in cotton wool. Instead, it's about keeping our landscape vibrant and ever-changing, allowing different plants to move around and find their own little preferred patches as these come and go in the natural cycle of birth, decay and renewal.

A raft of preventative measures

Today conservation is more about working on a large scale, providing opportunities for rare species across whole landscapes rather than pampering individual plants, or launching last-minute rescue missions to save species on the brink of extinction, such as lady's-slipper orchid (see opposite). Long before a plant declines to this point, however, a whole raft of conservation measures can be employed to keep species healthy in the wild, among the ever-changing community of wild things. The more essential steps include:

- Grazing in the right way with the most suitable livestock, as we saw with juniper (see pp.127–45).
- Removing scrub that might interfere with the growth of plants in the vicinity, such as Deptford pink (*Dianthus armeria*).
- Coppicing woodland by cutting back trees or shrubs to ground-level to keep the canopies open and enable sunlight to flood the forest floor where it can stimulate dormant seeds (see pp.201–3).
- Cutting hay to manage species-rich flower meadows that would otherwise run riot with overgrown grasses (see pp.212–15).
- Blocking drains and ditches to re-flood wetlands, which in turn encourages the growth of bog and wetland plants and allows peat to build up again.
- Controlling invasive species, such as rhododendron and New Zealand pigmyweed (see pp.159–71 and 182–6).

After the hay-cutting, Chris, Sally and Trevor collect bales of hay in an ancient meadow. As well as providing fodder for winter livestock feeding, hay-cutting encourages the growth of flower-rich meadows by keeping coarse grasses in check and preventing the build-up of nutrients that would otherwise allow brambles and scrub to take over. Hay, which is usually full of flower seeds, is often strewn on neighbouring fields to help spread wildflowers around.

Around the village of Muker in Yorkshire, large numbers of traditional hay meadows are managed in a way that works for both farming and wildlife. Following the July hay-cut, livestock graze each field heavily until they're removed in late winter and the meadows are 'shut up'. In response, the wildflowers put on a magnificent display, colouring the landscape with a haze of yellow buttercups.

Striking the right balance

Taking the longer view on a broader scale, we also need to restore the natural balance once again, giving wild things a chance to survive and thrive. Modern farming, which has impoverished traditional country habitats, such as meadows and cornfields, now has a role to play in restoring the delicate balance between agricultural production and natural life. It isn't about turning the clock back to a pre-industrial era, but rather about remembering the wider benefits of a countryside rich in life, and making room for all manner of plants, bugs, birds and mammals to flourish alongside modern technology. Clearly, neither the arable deserts devoted to a single crop, nor the acres of permanent pasture cultivated for a particular type of livestock, support a rich variety of wild things. One solution would be to encourage diversity of farming, with a mixture of crops and livestock, rather like traditional mixed farms (see pp.194–5). The ideal, though, would be to achieve exactly the right level and type of land management, with just enough grazing to keep nature in balance, because the reverse – too little grazing of pastures and meadows – would be just as bad for our wildlife as too much grazing. Similarly, leaving most woodlands untouched would be as unproductive as felling them entirely.

Nurturing the wild things

It's equally important to protect and encourage our plant life in rare or exceptional natural habitats. In the British Isles we're fortunate that some very special plant havens, including Important Plant Areas (IPAs), remain under our protection. Abounding in a rich variety of rare plants, IPAs are renowned for their exceptional wild plant populations (see overleaf). The ultimate aim will be to conserve the best sites, such as IPAs, and restore the rest of the landscape, recreating and reconnecting these vibrant tracts of land so that wild things can move freely around the countryside once more. The process of restoration and recreation can't be forced with quick planting, though. Ancient woodlands and grasslands should be left to regenerate naturally over time, allowing individual species to move in and find their own place. In this way, these special habitats will retain their local character and be able to build up the complex web of life that defines them.

In our own gardens, too, we can help protect our wild things by curbing the spread of destructive non-natives. We should try, for example, to prevent invasive species, such as Spanish bluebell, from escaping into the wild by discarding them responsibly (see p.70). Even better, we should simply stop growing troublesome species altogether and plant alternatives that don't cause problems if they escape (see chapter 5).

Native woodlands take time to develop and regenerate naturally – nature can't be forced. Here, the mixture of trees of different ages, along with the lichen- and moss-covered trunks and branches, the ground flora and underground fungi, have all matured gradually over decades and even centuries.

FIVE BOTANICAL HAVENS

The crown jewels of our botanical heritage, Important Plant Areas (IPAs) shelter rare and varied species and habitats. Valued internationally for their exceptional plant populations, IPAs are now being recognized worldwide in a programme led by the plant conservation charity Plantlife (see pp.244–5). In the UK, 150 IPAs have already been identified, including the following five.

1 Cairngorms, Scotland

At more than 1,220m high, the Cairngorms are the tallest mountains in the British Isles. Their height and distance from the sea produces low winter temperatures, encouraging the most arctic vegetation found anywhere in the country. Many arctic-alpines flourish here, such as woolly willow (*Salix lanata*) and the highly rare alpine fleabane (*Erigeron borealis*). Thanks to snow-beds lying late on the slopes, the Cairngorms also shelter many important mosses and liverworts (see pp.148–9).

2 Yorkshire Dales, England

The Great Scar Limestone so redolent of the Dales was laid down on seabeds some 300 million years ago. The characteristic ridged texture of today's limestone pavements was formed during the last Ice Age, *c*.2.58 million years ago, when glaciers scraped away the surface of the seabed, exposing the natural joints in the underlying rock, which was then eroded by slightly acidic rain. The thin soils covering the rock today are home to a rich diversity of lime-loving grasses, ferns and wildflowers for which the limestone country of the Dales is justly renowned.

3 Ranscombe Farm, England

Famous for its rare wildflowers, such as lady orchid (*Orchis purpurea*), Ranscombe Farm is Plantlife's largest English nature reserve, covering more than 250 hectares. Recently declared a country park, it includes some of our richest arable habitats, extensive ancient woodlands and fragments of chalk grassland. Much of the reserve lies within the Cobham Woods Site of Special Scientific Interest, while the whole farm forms part of the Kent Downs Area of Outstanding Natural Beauty.

4 Gower Peninsula, Wales

From limestone cliffs to dune grasslands, from open moorlands to ash woodlands – there is something here for every plant lover. The cliffs are home to several specialized species that can survive sea winds and salt spray, such as yellow whitlowgrass (*Draba aizoides*) and goldilocks aster (*Aster linosyris*), while the dune grasslands shelter more than 250 species of flowering plant, including the rare fen orchid (*Liparis loeselii*). Gower's extensive woodlands, too, offer spectacular displays of wildflowers.

5 Upper Lough Erne, Ireland

A large freshwater system formed from a series of flooded mounds in the River Erne, the Upper Lough is a complex of islands, bays and lakes bordered by damp pastures, fens and reed swamps, as well as ample alder, willow and oak forests. The surrounding parkland is renowned for its ancient trees and associated rare lichens.

The British Isles offers a dynamic diversity of IPAs across the country, ranging from freshwater fens to coastal dunes, from lime-rich pavements to mountain snow-beds.

BELOW Like Chris, the plants on Salisbury Plain in Wiltshire soak up the midday sun. Unlike Chris, though, viper's-bugloss (Echium vulgare) can convert the sun's energy into sugar and then turn it into nectar to feed pollinating bees.

OPPOSITE Sally searches for white-flowered wild carrot (Daucus carota) on Salisbury Plain. Though small and tough compared to our modern garden carrot, the root of wild carrot was an important food source for Iron Age people – evidence of our long history with wild plants.

MORE THAN WILD WALLPAPER

Our relationship with wild plants has changed dramatically within a generation. Although our parents and grandparents were much more likely to have known the names of many wild plants around them, today the average adult in the British Isles often can't recognize more than five different wild species.

To some extent plants have become a bit like pretty wallpaper in our lives – a pleasant but out-of-focus background for the birds, butterflies, bees and other beasties that we cherish in the countryside. In reality, though, plants provide much more than a pleasing backdrop – quite the reverse, in fact, as they perform many roles that are central to the survival of other wild things. First and foremost, they provide the fundamental energy and primary life support for most species on earth: it's only plants that can capture energy from sunlight to create the sugar that fuels the majority of life on earth; equally, it's only plants that release oxygen into the atmosphere, which supports most wild things on the planet (see p.43).

TIME TO STAND AND STARE ...

In our busy modern lives, with computers, mobile phones and social media making non-stop demands on our time and attention, it's easy to forget the little things – the flowers and butterflies, bugs and beetles, lichens and mosses all around us. Yet our world depends on countless millions of these tiny jewels of life that strung together make up the bigger web of life. When you next step outside, pause to look out for some of them, such as morning dewdrops suspended on the gossamer threads of a spider's cobweb (right). Scientific studies have shown that spending just five minutes a day with nature reaps huge rewards on our health and wellbeing. Perhaps we owe the little things a few moments of our time.

On the Isle of Jura, Scotland, a damp coastal meadow on Ardfernal Hill is splashed with vibrant purple loosestrife (Lythrum salicaria) in a froth of meadowsweet (Filipendula ulmaria). Although often overlooked, almost all our landscapes are clothed in a rich mantle of plants, providing much more than just an attractive backdrop to our lives.

Crucially, too, plants form the basic building blocks of most habitats – as a glance at almost any will quickly reveal – whether marshes or forests, grasslands or heaths (see chapters 2, 4 and 6). In each habitat, plants play a vital role in maintaining a healthy balance within a complex web of life. Just think of a few essential tasks performed by plants that often go unnoticed – they keep water clean wherever it runs, from mountain springs to rivers rushing out to sea; they help prevent flooding and soil erosion; and they soak up and store huge reserves of atmospheric carbon dioxide, reducing climate warming.

As if that were not enough, different plants also provide shelter and cover for many wild things, including ourselves. Indeed, probably more than any other species, we've always banked on plants in countless ways. Throughout history, different cultures have relied on timber, straw, fibres and leaves for essential

shelter and cover; on fruits, roots and seeds for vital nutritious
food and drink. We've also benefited from medicinal herbs,
refreshing teas and reviving spices and spirits derived from
the various leaves, berries and seeds of plants (see pp.43, 131).

Last but not least, all types of foliage and flowers play a subtle
but important part in everyone's life, both private and public,
marking special moments and rites of passage – from a birthday
rose to a Remembrance poppy, from a laurel wreath to a mistletoe.

Our landscape is clothed in a rich mantle of plants. We can
see them year after year, reliable and welcome harbingers of the
turning seasons. Take away all other forms of wildlife for just
a few minutes and the countryside would look pretty much the
same. Take away the plants, and the landscape would be barren
and desolate – just bare rock and soil. The role played by plants
in our lives and landscape is incomparable.

HOW TO GET INVOLVED

Whether you're keen to hone your field skills, to track down rare plants and campaign for threatened species, or simply to ramble at will through remote and beautiful nature havens, why not team up with fellow plant lovers at the British Isles' leading botanical societies?

Welsh poppies flourishing on the cool, damp slopes of Cwm Idwal in Snowdonia, North Wales.

PLANT GROUP	NUMBER OF SPECIES IN THE BRITISH ISLES
Vascular plants (flowering plants, trees, ferns and horsetails, see p.43)	2,951 (1,407 native)
Bryophytes (liverworts and mosses, see p.43)	1,134
Lichens (see p.45)	1,835
Fungi (see p.45)	15,000+

The Botanical Society of the British Isles (BSBI)

For people who're passionate about plants, the BSBI offers many opportunities to learn more, including field trips, conferences and a range of publications, such as plant distribution atlases and the *New Journal of Botany*.

Since its inception in 1836, when it was founded as the Botanical Society of London, the BSBI has grown to become the country's leading charitable voluntary organization, promoting the study and enjoyment of British and Irish flowering plants. Through its varied activities, the BSBI aims not only to improve our understanding of wild plants, but also to support and encourage research and conservation.

From its earliest days, the organization has welcomed both professional and amateur members, who are kept informed by a newsletter three times a year and can benefit from the help of our expert county recorders and national referees in identifying wild plants. To find out more, see their website:
I http://www.bsbi.org.uk
E info@bsbi.org.uk

Plantlife

Wildflowers, plants and fungi play a fundamental role in the lives of all wild things, and their colour and character light up our landscapes. Without our help, though, this priceless natural heritage is in danger of being lost. Plantlife speaks up for the British Isles' wild plants – from the open spaces of their nature reserves to the corridors of government, the conservation charity sets out to raise the profile of all wild plants, to celebrate their beauty and to protect their future. The organization's expert botanists identify and conserve landscapes of exceptional botanical importance; rescue wild plants from the brink of extinction; and work to ensure that common plants don't become rare in the wild.

In addition to Plantlife's direct conservation work, the organization manages nature reserves, influences policy and legislation, and runs events and activities for people to learn about and celebrate their local wild plants. Plantlife's patron is HRH The Prince of Wales.

Why not join Plantlife in enjoying the best that nature has to offer – visit one of their nature reserves, take part in a guided walk, or sign up for the Wildflowers Count survey? As a Plantlife member, you'll receive a magazine three times a year, along with invitations to events and a free guide to Plantlife's nature reserves. To learn more about Plantlife, see their website:
I http://www.plantlife.org.uk
E enquiries@plantlife.org.uk

The British Lichen Society (BLS)

Everyone with a passion for lichens is welcome at the BLS – whether you are a complete beginner or someone with a lifetime's experience of lichenology, you'll find plenty to stimulate and develop your interest in lichens.

The BLS supports lichenology throughout the world, but with a special emphasis on the British Isles. Their aims are to promote and advance the teaching and study of lichens; to encourage and actively support the conservation of lichens and their habitats; and to raise public awareness of the beauty of lichens and of their importance as indicators of the health of our environment. To these ends, the BLS runs field trips, workshops and recording projects, which are open to all members.

To discover more about the extraordinary world of lichens, why not join the BLS? The member's magazine *The Bulletin* is packed with information about lichens, lichenologists and events, while the organization's highly regarded scientific journal, *The Lichenologist*, features more specialized articles. You can find out more about the BLS on their website:
I http://www.britishlichensociety.org.uk
E c.ellis@rbge.org.uk

The British Bryological Society (BBS)

At the BBS, there's something for everyone who's interested in learning about liverworts and mosses (bryophytes). The society promotes the study of bryophytes with a full programme of field trips, practical workshop weekends, paper-reading circles and recording and research projects. The BBS also produces a range of publications, including a lively bi-annual membership magazine, *The Bulletin*, which is full of news, notices and articles of general interest. If you'd like to learn more about bryophytes, please visit their website:
I http://www.britishbryologicalsociety.org.uk

INDEX

Acknowledgements

From germination to flowering, this book has involved many people who deserve my thanks. Firstly, I'm very grateful to Cwmni Da television production company for the opportunity to appear in the *Wild Things* television series and to write this accompanying book; and to both Channel 4 and Transworld Publishers for believing in the project. The production team at Cwmni Da were inspirational throughout, bringing the *Wild Things* series to fruition with thorough research and good humour at every stage.

The same goes for my fellow contributors, Sally Eaton, Chris Myers and television producer, Clare Jones, all of whom provided wonderful material for their sections (see below). Lottie the Labrador, too, posed perfectly for photographs at every opportunity.

At Cwmni Da, special thanks to Neville Hughes, who oversaw the whole project; Fiona Pitts, who tracked down many elusive photographs; and Huw Maredudd, who co-ordinated the production of the maps, the designs of which are thanks to the talent of Roughcollie.tv, motion and interactive design.

At Transworld Publishers, my thanks go to Michelle Signore, Editorial Director, for setting the book so firmly on track, and to Isobel Gillan, whose inspirational design has enlivened the pages throughout. A big bunch of flowers goes to the project editor, Belinda Wilkinson, who worked tirelessly pruning and nurturing to produce beautiful and readable prose.

Thank you to Plantlife, who have patiently supported me throughout the entire growing season of *Wild Things*. The various botanical societies have also nourished the project, especially Kevin Walker and Tom Humphrey at the BSBI. In addition, Kevin provided valuable botanical comment on the draft manuscript. Thanks also to Fred Rumsey and Colin Newlands for their help and botanical expertise. Chris Preston and David Pearman also deserve a special mention for the seedlings created for this book, while we co-edited the *New Atlas of the British and Irish Flora* in 2002.

Throughout the filming and writing for the project, family and friends have been unwavering in their support, both watering and feeding me at every turn over the past few months.

Finally, but perhaps most importantly, I thank all those enthusiastic volunteers who spend their spare time outdoors finding, identifying and recording all our wild things. Without them, there would be no stories to tell – *Diolch yn fawr iawn* (thank you very much).

TREVOR DINES

Text Contributors

Dr Trevor Dines: pp.24–44, 46–9, 52–3, 56–67, 70–3, 76–81, 85–7, 90–101, 104–7, 110–13, 116–23, 126–47, 150–55, 158–77, 180–9, 194–217, 220–21, 224–37, 240–3.

Sally Eaton: pp.45, 50–1, 72–3, 82–4, 108–9, 114–15, 118, 148–9, 178–9, 218–19.

Clare Jones: pp.8–21, 68–9, 84, 102–3, 132–3, 190–91.

One of the Cwmni Da producers on the *Wild Things* television series, Clare is also a professional travel writer and photographer.

Chris Myers: pp.6–7

Text Credits

William Henry Davies: p.241, line 1 ('… time to stand and stare …'), from 'Leisure' in *Songs Of Joy and Others* (1911).

Map Credits

Plant distribution map data reproduced courtesy of the Botanical Society of the British Isles (BSBI) and the British Lichen Society (BLS).

Map Coordinators: Tom Humphrey and Huw Maredudd.

Map designer: Roughcollie.tv, motion and interactive design.

Picture Credits

Abbreviations

Cwmni Da CD
Trevor Dines TD
Eira Wyn Jones EWJ
Neville Hughes NH
Nature Picture Library NPL
Plantlife PL
Science Photo Library SPL

TRANSWORLD PUBLISHERS
61–63 Uxbridge Road, London W5 5SA
A Random House Group Company
www.transworldbooks.co.uk

First published in Great Britain
in 2012 by Channel 4 Books,
an imprint of Transworld Publishers.

This book is published to accompany the *Wild Things*
television series produced by Cwmni Da.

General Editor: Neville Hughes
Project Editor: Belinda Wilkinson
Designer: Isobel Gillan

A CIP catalogue record for this book
is available from the British Library.

ISBN 9781905026999

Addresses for Random House Group Ltd companies outside the UK can be found at:
www.randomhouse.co.uk
The Random House Group Ltd Reg. No. 954009

The Random House Group Limited supports the Forest Stewardship Council (FSC®), the
leading international forest-certification organization. Our books carrying the FSC label are
printed on FSC®-certified paper. FSC is the only forest-certification scheme endorsed by
the leading environmental organizations, including Greenpeace. Our paper procurement
policy can be found at www.randomhouse.co.uk/environment.

Printed and bound in Great Britain by
Butler Tanner & Dennis Ltd

2 4 6 8 10 9 7 5 3 1